A Field Guide to ^(some of) the Peoples of the British Isles

A Field Guide to

Some of

THE PEOPLES

of the British Isles

Chelsea Renton

ONEWORLD

for **Annie and Orde**
don't worry, you're not in it

Additional species can be spotted in
The Oldie, where the Field Guide has
been a regular feature since 2017

A Oneworld Book

First published by Oneworld
Publications, 2019

Copyright © Chelsea Renton 2019

The moral right of Chelsea Renton
to be identified as the Author of
this work has been asserted by her
in accordance with the Copyright,
Designs, and Patents Act 1988

ISBN 978-1-78607-692-2
eISBN 978-1-78607-693-9

Designed by Grita Rose-Innes

Reprography by Martin Chapman

Printed and bound in China by
C&C Offset Printing Ltd

Oneworld Publications
10 Bloomsbury Street
London WC1B 3SR
England

CONTENTS

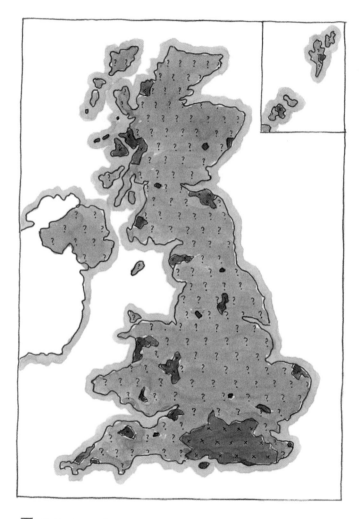

 Field observation

Wild speculation

INTRODUCTION

The idea for this book came about while bird-watching
in Scotland. As I flicked through a guidebook failing
to identify seabirds, I found myself distracted by the people
on the beach – some picnicking noisily, a few shivering in
the surf and one solitary walker occasionally stooping to
examine an object in the tideline. I instantly thought of the
fun I could have categorising friends, neighbours and even
strangers, according to diet, plumage and behaviour.

I rushed home delighted to have stumbled across an idea
that would allow me to spend many hours bent over my
drawing board, with just a dip pen and paper, happily
giggling at my own jokes. I realised though, quite early on,
that my field of observation is limited. Living in the South
East, I am familiar with the activated-charcoal smoothie
drinkers of Brighton, but know less of the legendary hen
parties of Newcastle, the curry-milers of Manchester and
the offshore workers of Aberdeen. The British Isles are rich
in wonderful species and I look forward to observing them
all one day, making sweeping generalisations and giving
them a big nose.

In the meantime, I should say that any similarity to people
alive or dead is entirely intentional. If you think it's you,
then it probably is.

Chelsea Renton

BUILDER / THERAPIST / HAIRSTYLIST
ARTIST / LOCAL COUNCILLOR
HIPSTER / PARENT / VICAR / FOODIE (widespread)

BUILDER (traditional)

♂ only

Observing a Builder (traditional) in the field:

morning

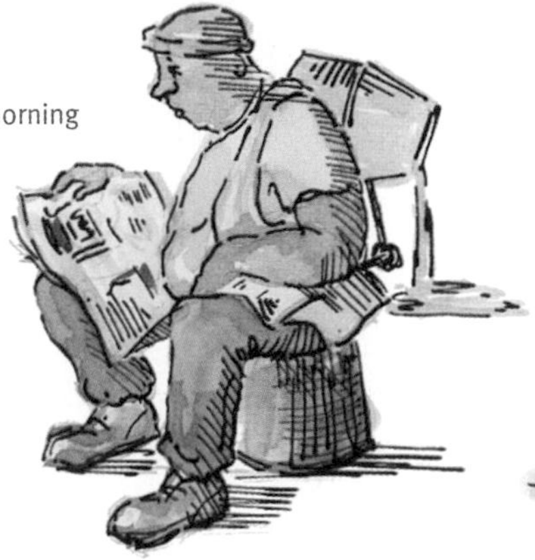

lunchtime

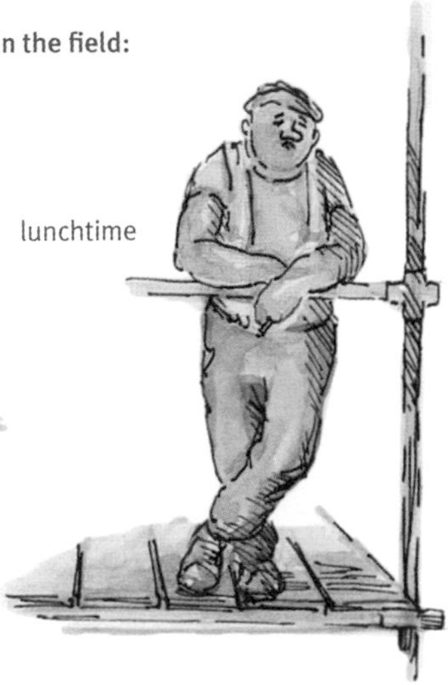

afternoon

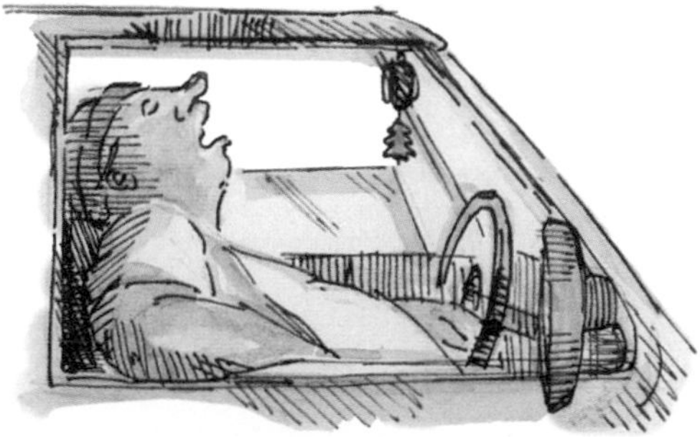

Staple diet:

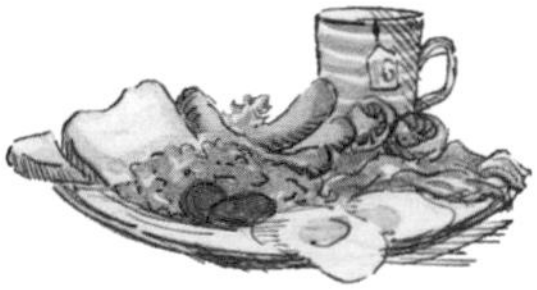

at rest

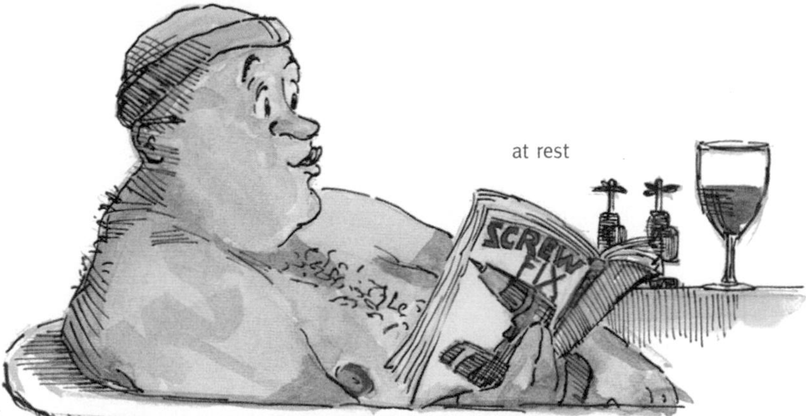
SCREW
FIX

BUILDER (gentleman)

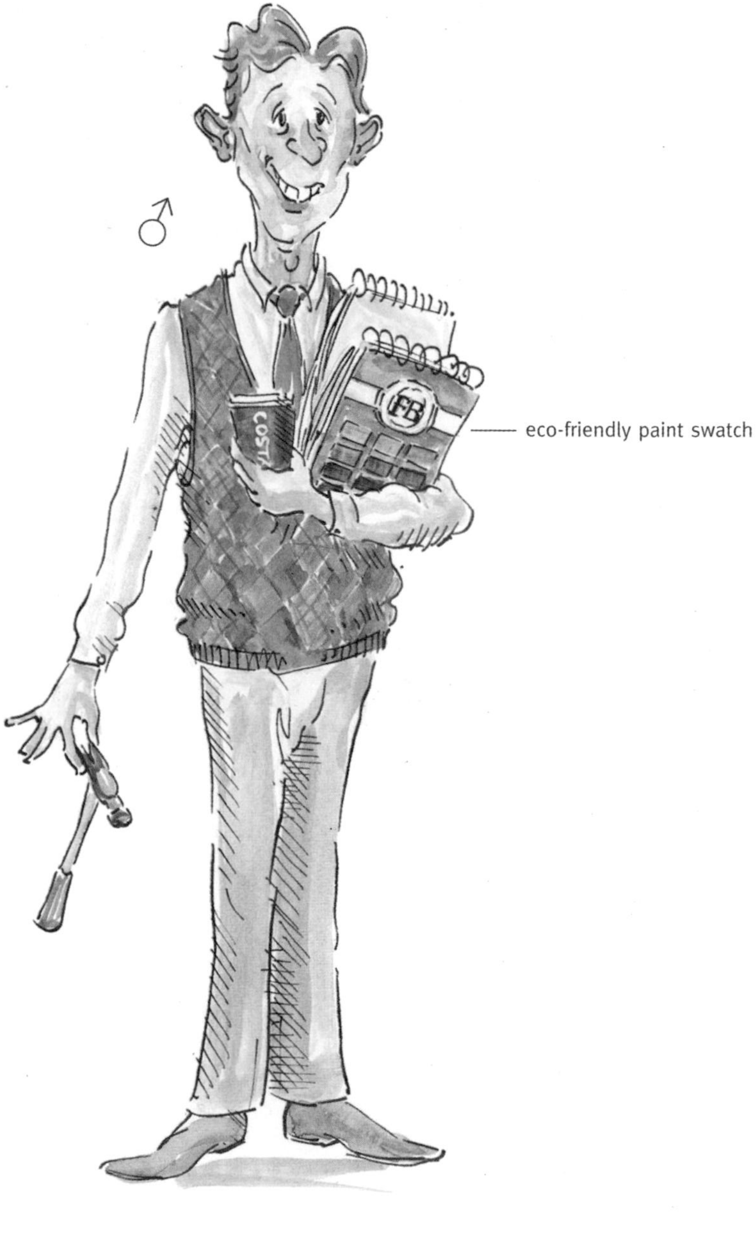

♂
COSTA
FB
eco-friendly paint swatch

BUILDER **(Polish*)**

*endangered

Common trait: all builders liable to disappear overnight to "finish off the last job"

THERAPIST

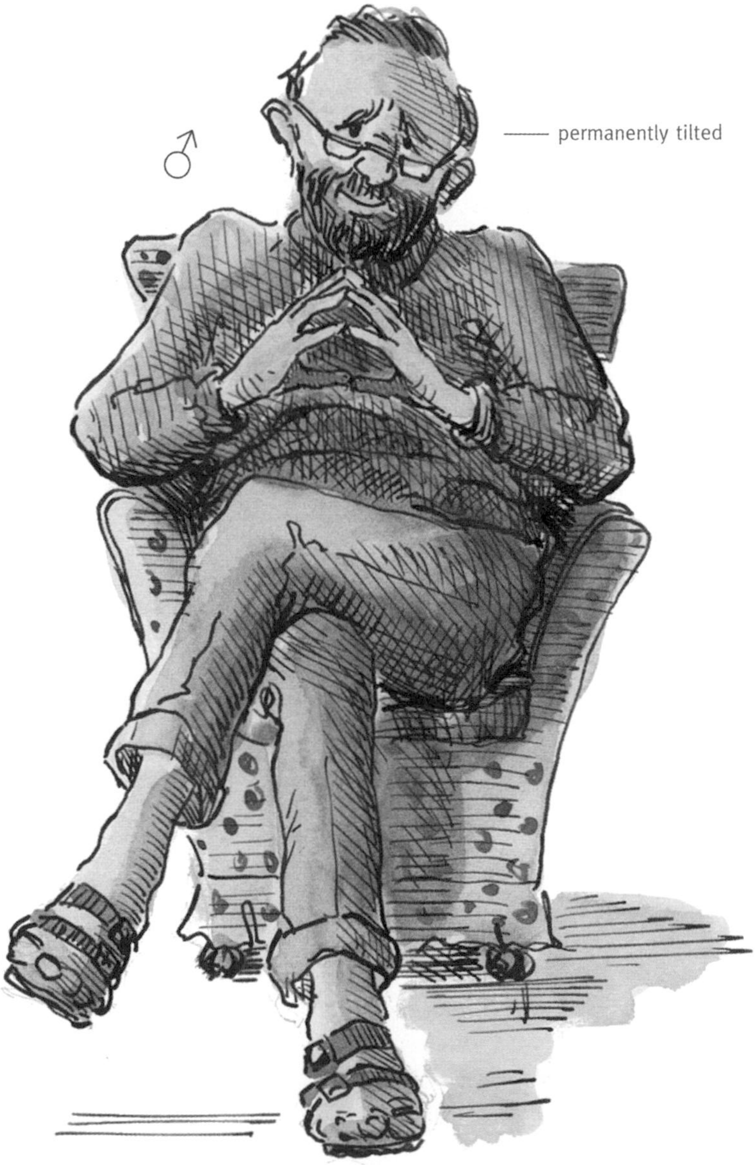

♂
permanently tilted

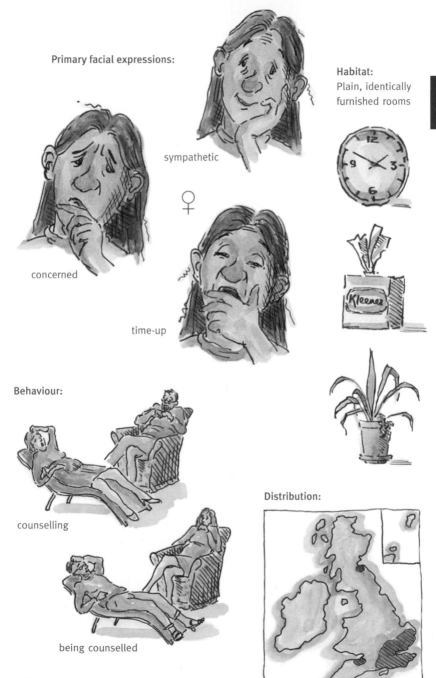

Primary facial expressions:

sympathetic

concerned

time-up

Habitat:
Plain, identically furnished rooms

Behaviour:

counselling

being counselled

Distribution:

Voice: low repetitive "hmmm...hmmm...hmmm..."

HAIRSTYLIST

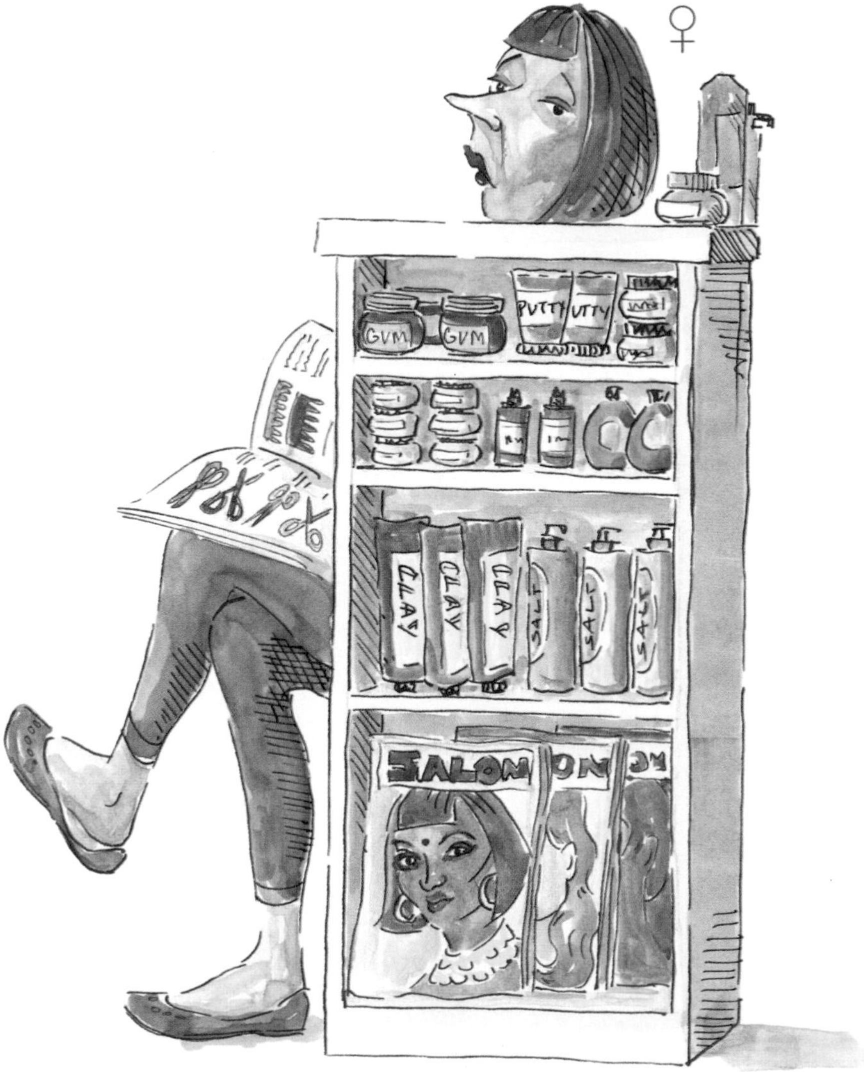
GUM
GUM
PUTTY
UTTY
CLAY
CLAY
CLAY
SALT
SALT
SALT
SALON

Interaction with other species:

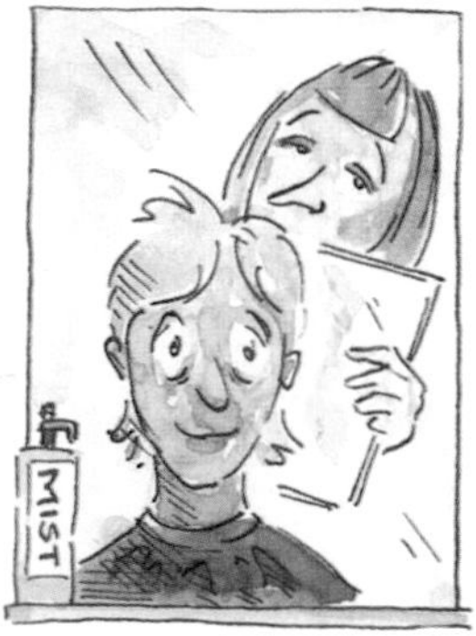
MIST

gamine

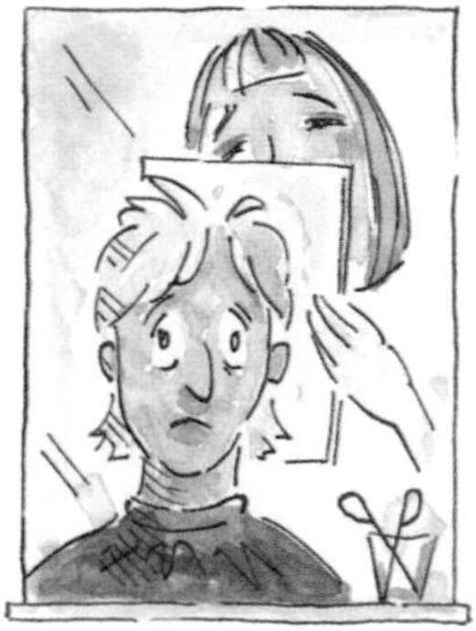

feathered

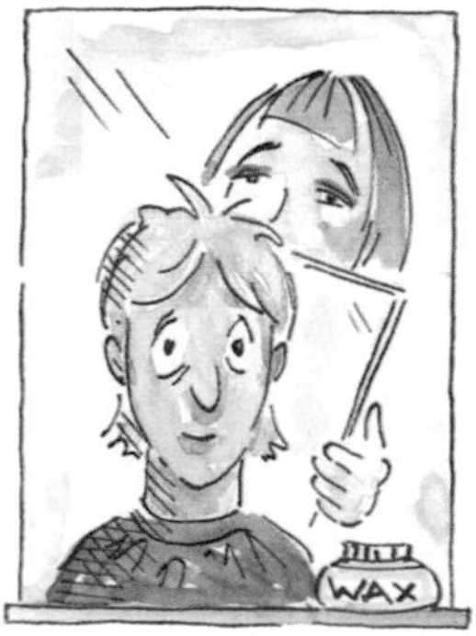
WAX

layered

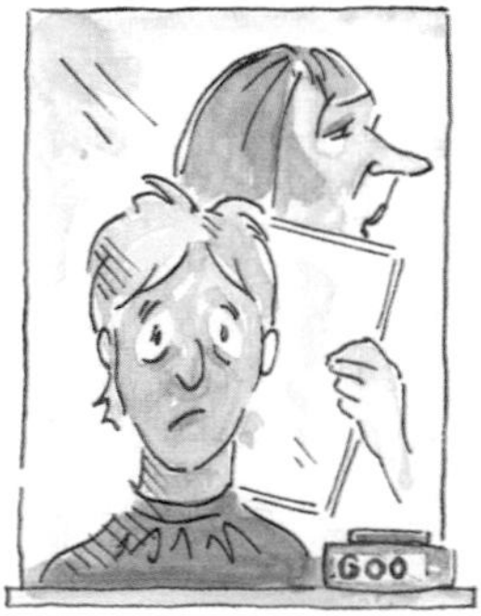
GOO

like last time

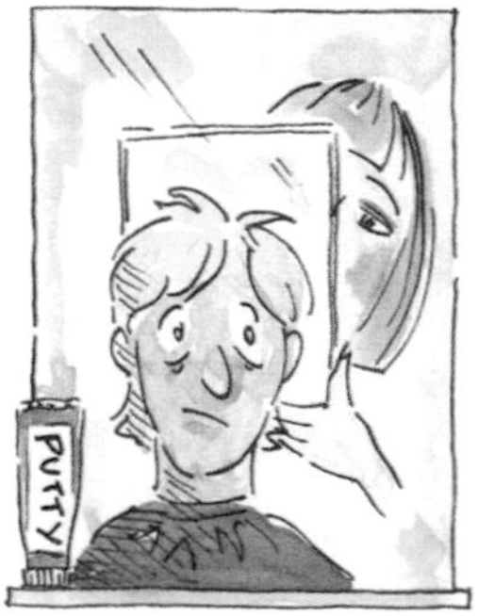
PUTTY

like Robin Wright in *House of Cards*

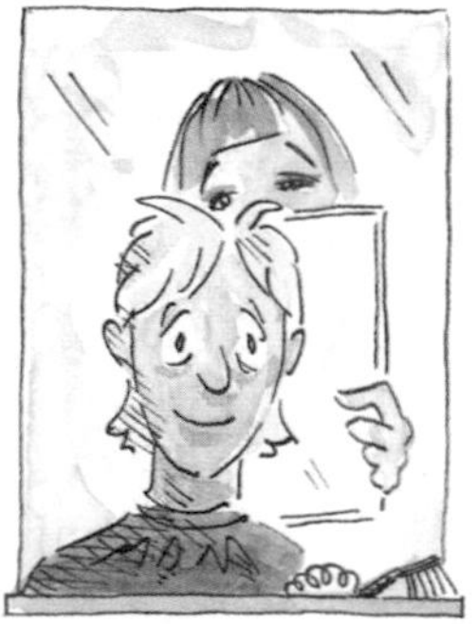

get-up-and-go

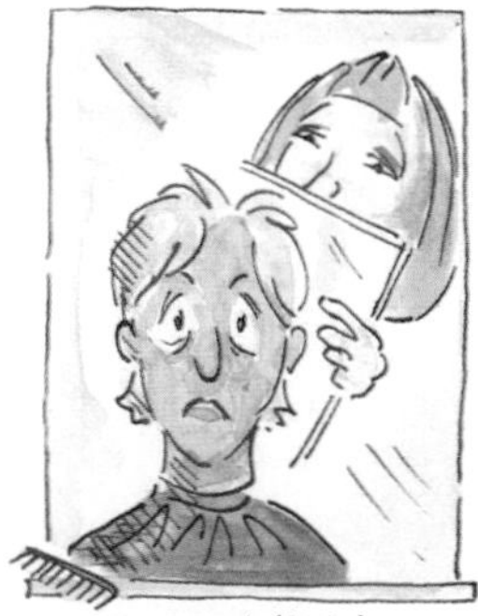

textured (£160)

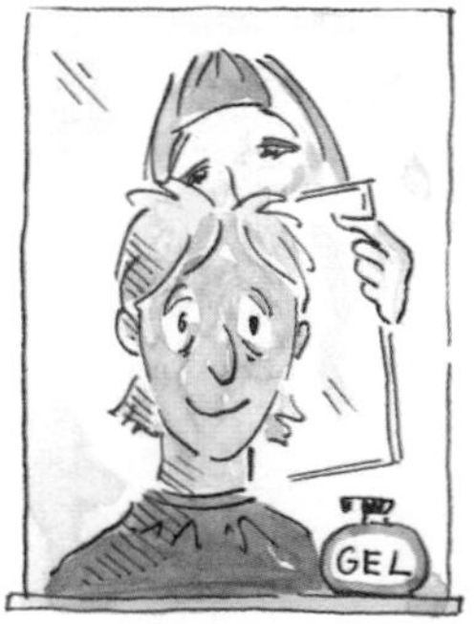
GEL

choppy

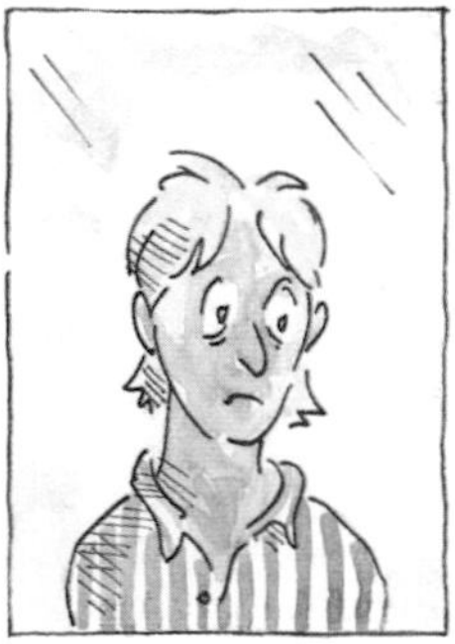

missed appointment

ARTIST (amateur)

Plumage:

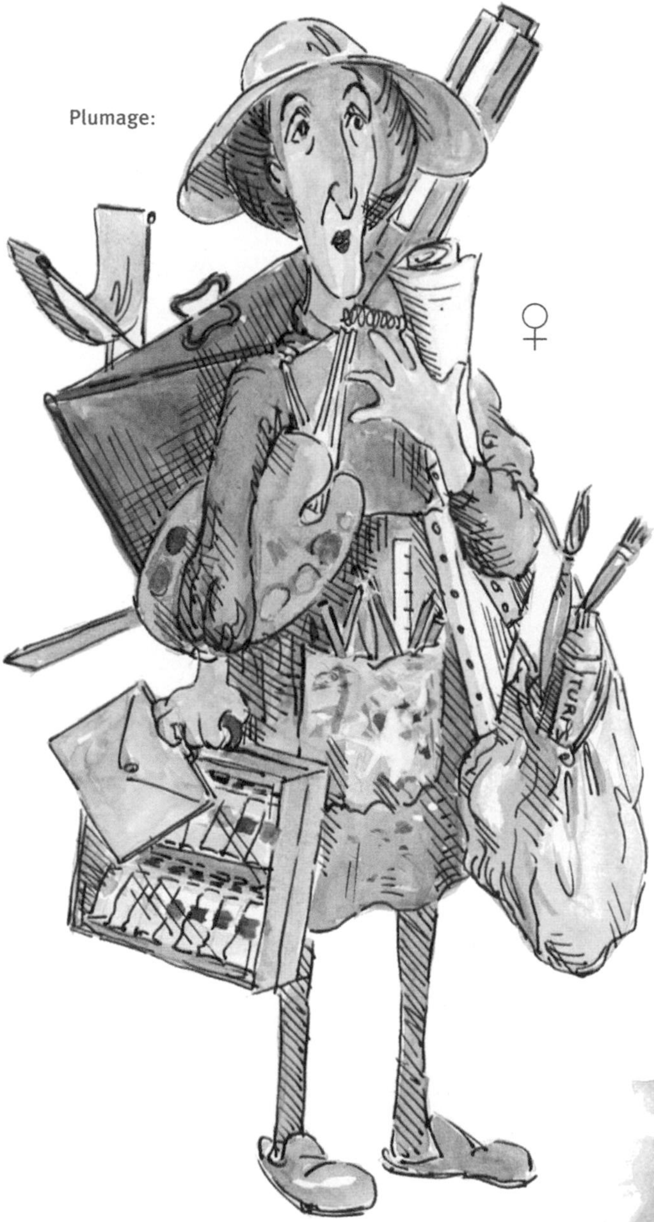

♀

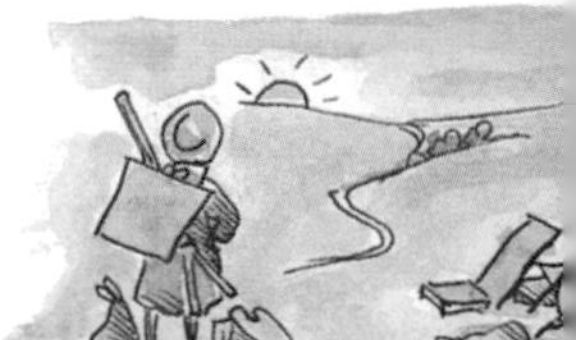

Facial expressions:

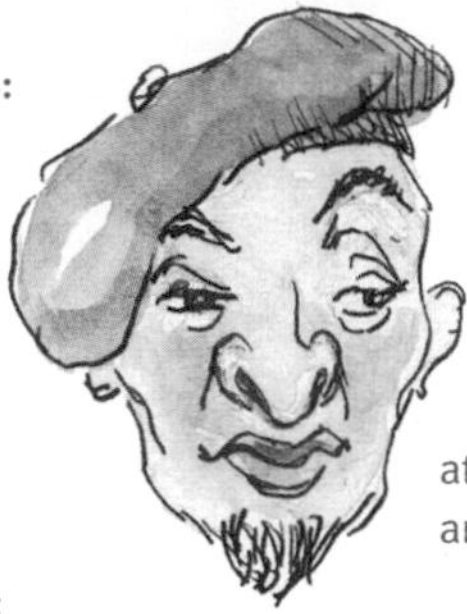

at local
art show

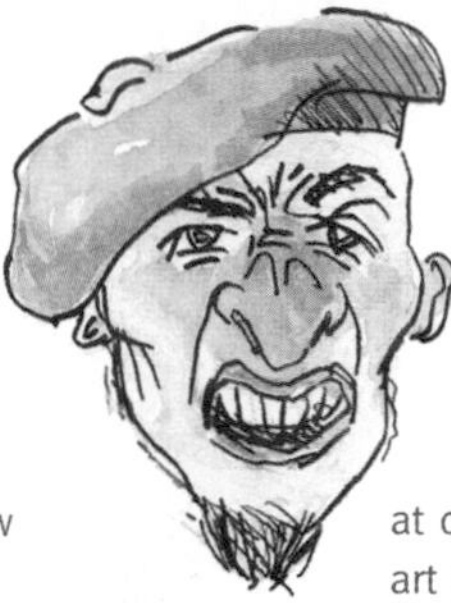

at conceptual
art exhibition

Often seen with:

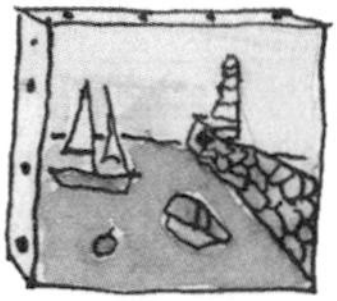

Harbour at dawn

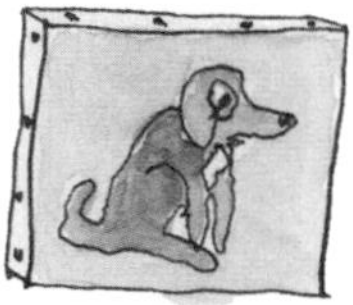

Pip

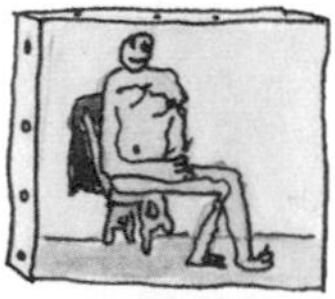

The red chemise

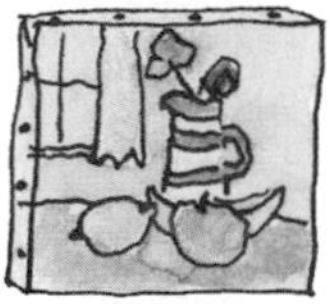

Still life

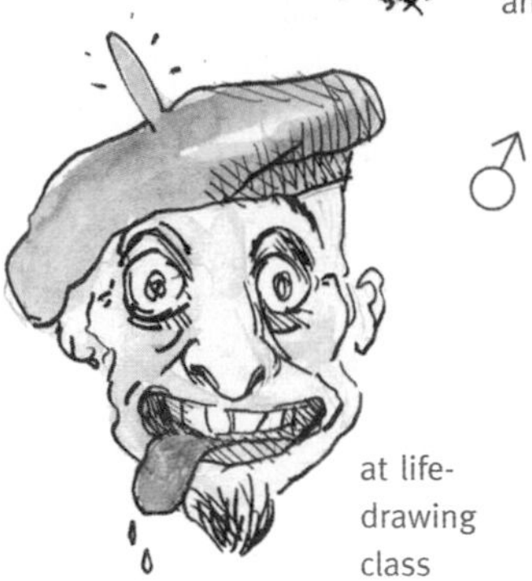
♂

at life-
drawing
class

Distribution:

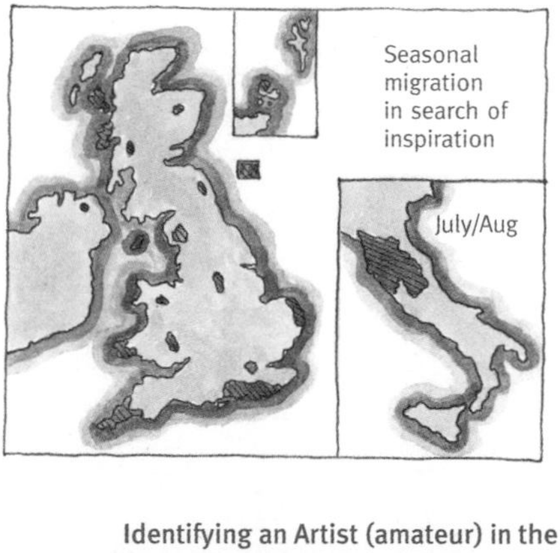
Seasonal
migration
in search of
inspiration
July/Aug

Identifying an Artist (amateur) in the field:

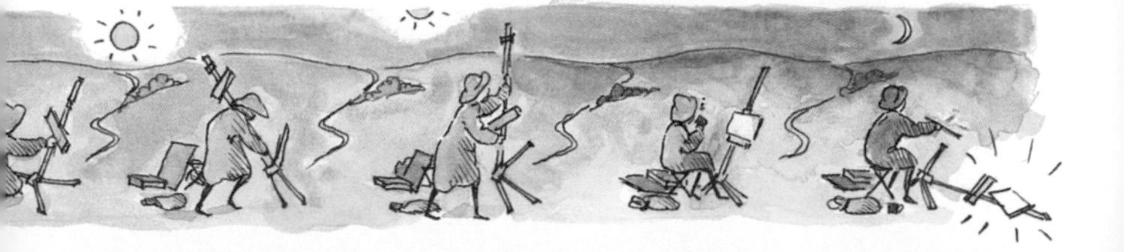

LOCAL COUNCILLOR

Alpha ♂

ribbon ready

Bait:

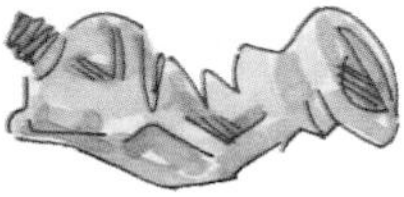

single-use plastic

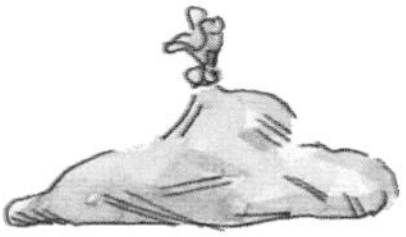

dog poo bag

Flocking:

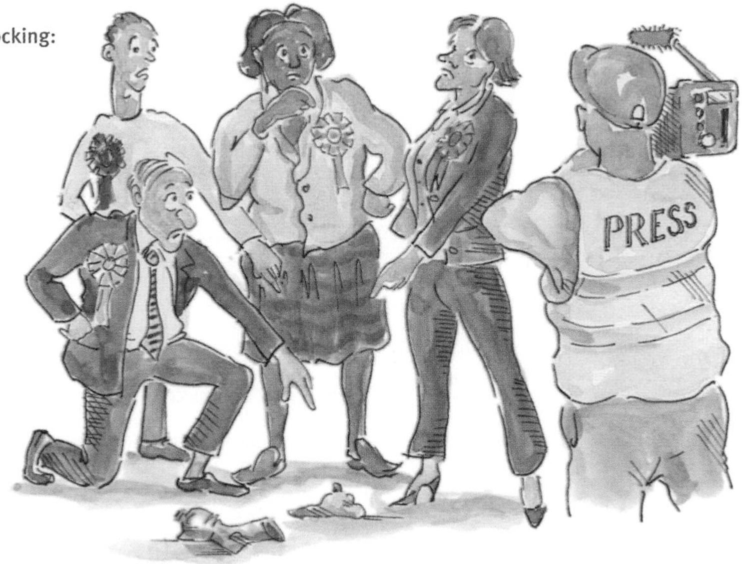
PRESS

Distribution:

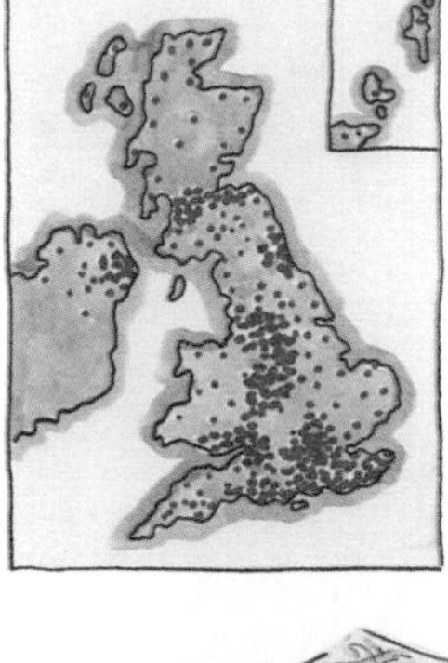

Spoor:

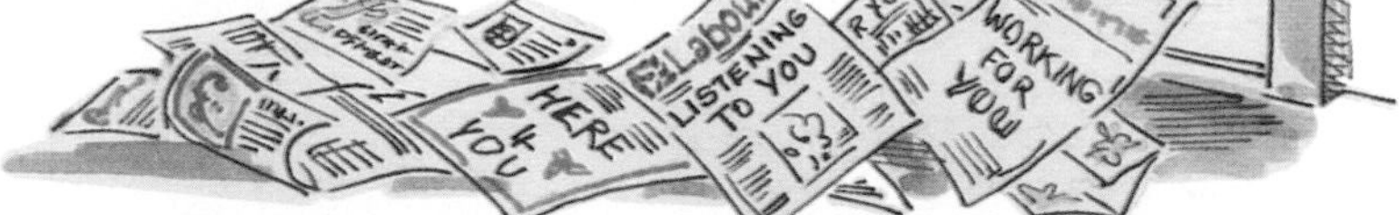
Labour
LISTENING TO YOU
HERE 4 YOU
WORKING FOR YOU

HIPSTER

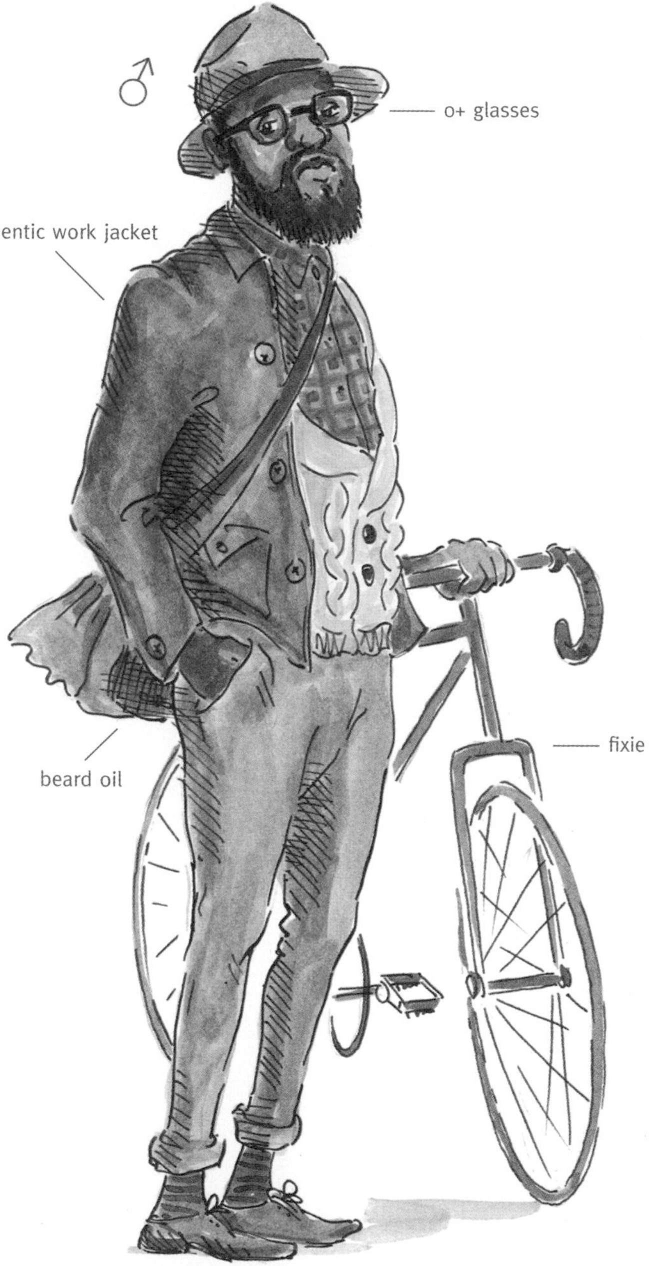
♂
o+ glasses
authentic work jacket
beard oil
fixie

Variations in plumage:

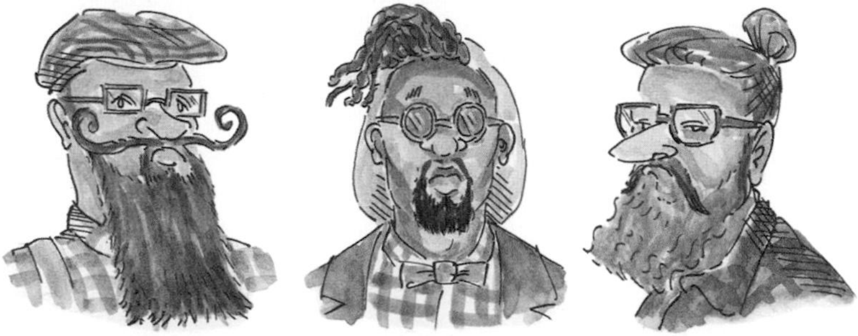

Flocking:

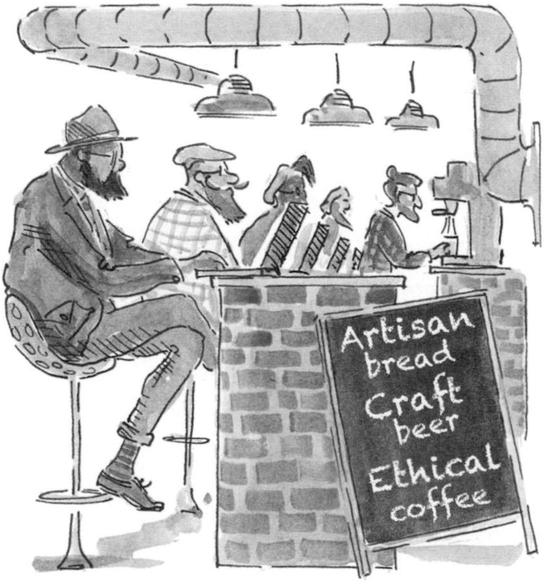
Artisan bread
Craft beer
Ethical coffee

Distribution:

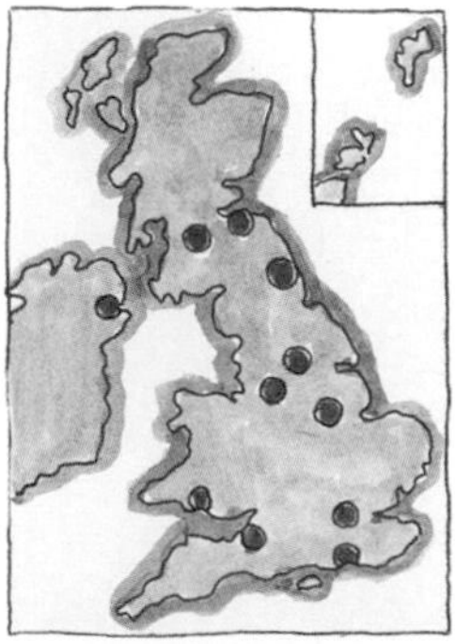

Behaviour:

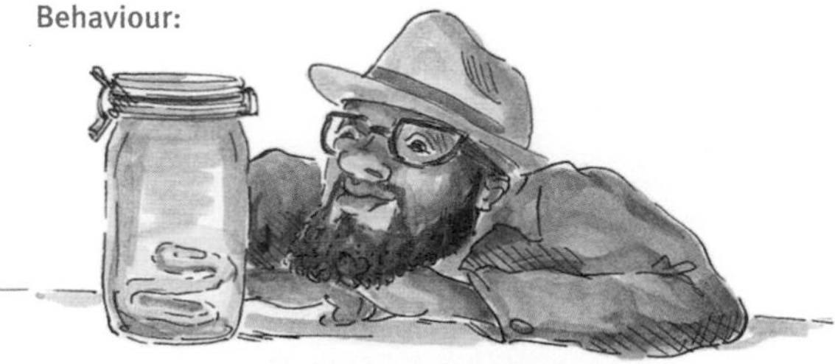

fomenting a new culture

PARENT (single mum)

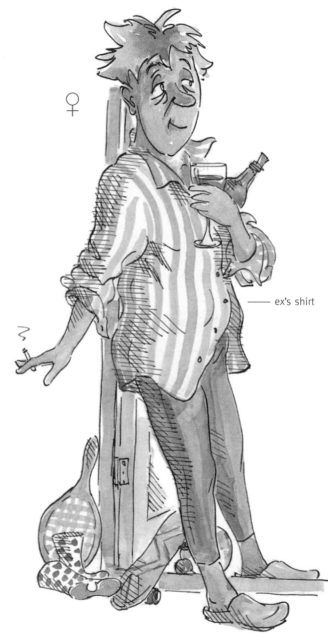

♀

ex's shirt

Observing a Parent (single mum) in the field:

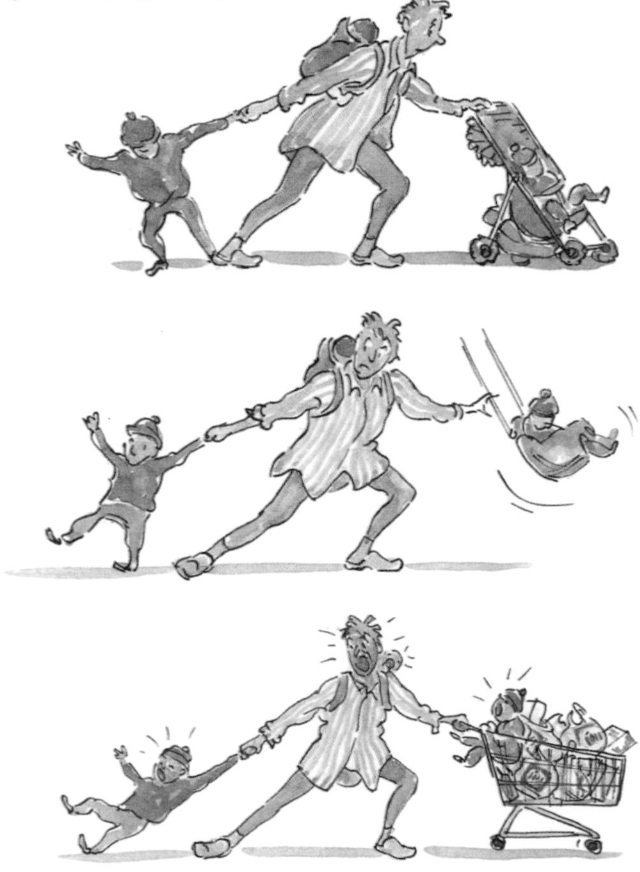

Mate (potential):

Staple diet:

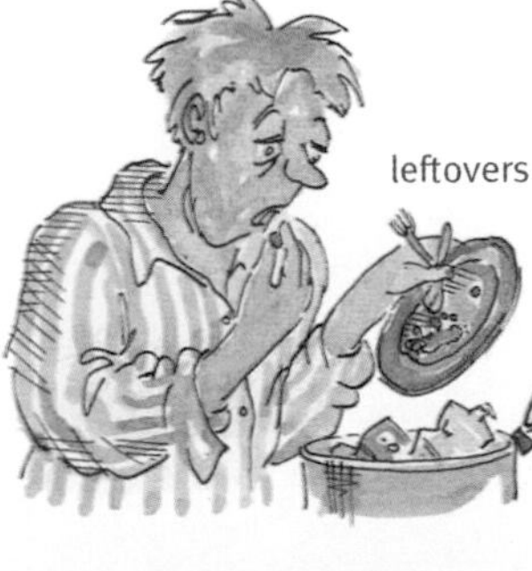
leftovers

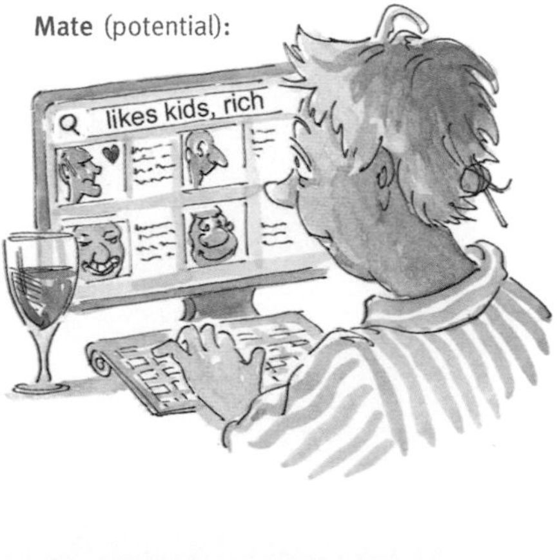
likes kids, rich

PARENT (single dad)

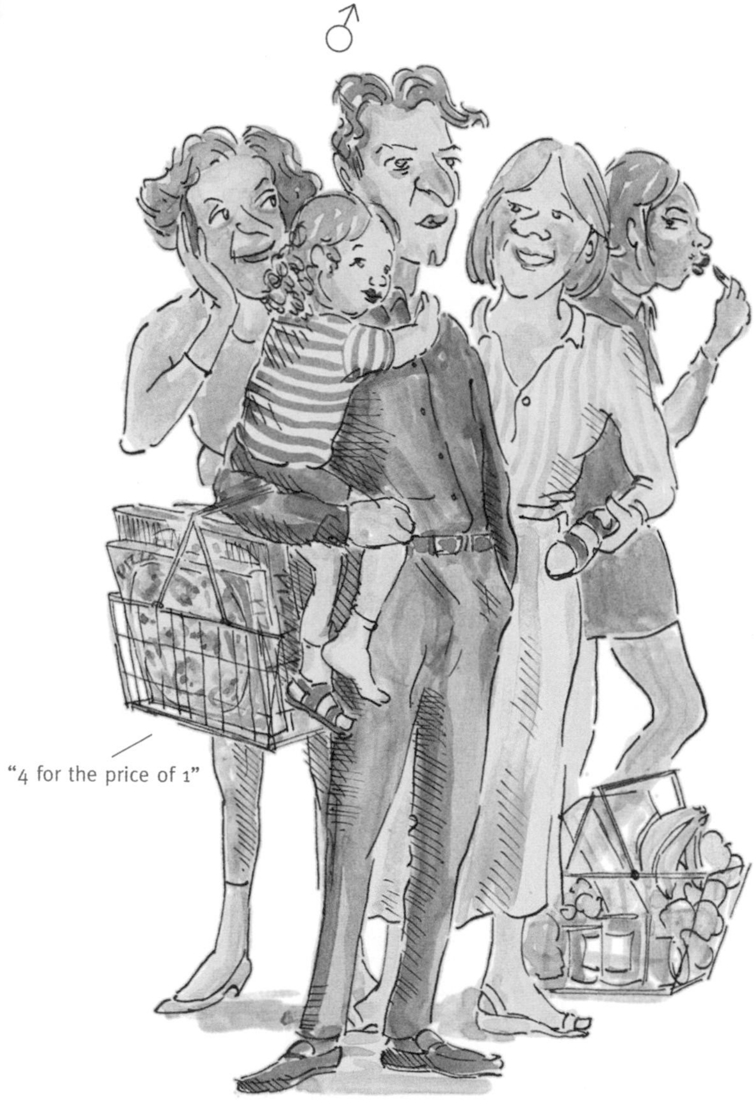
♂
"4 for the price of 1"

(yummy mummy)

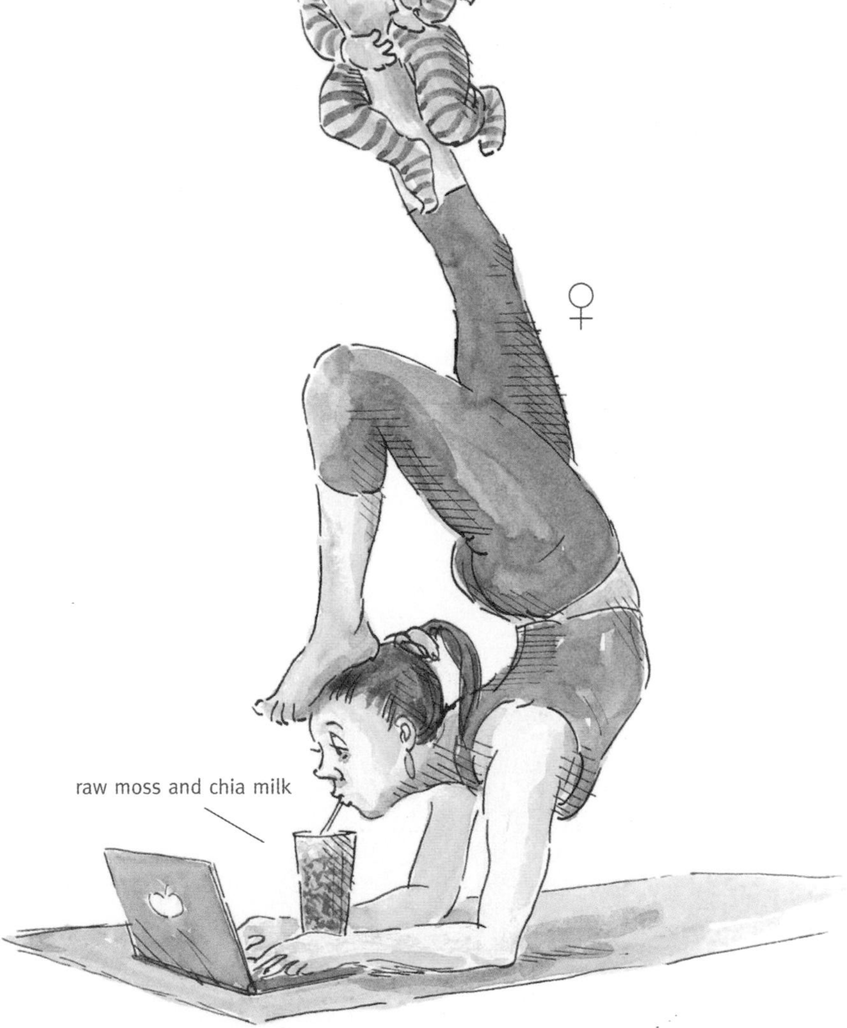
♀
raw moss and chia milk

PARENT (empty nester)

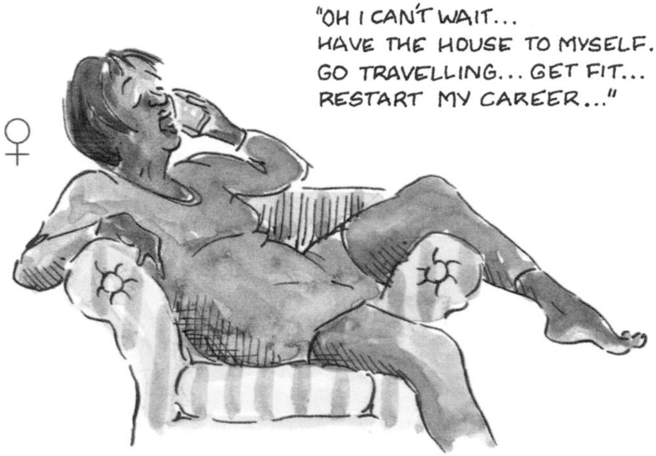
"OH I CAN'T WAIT...
HAVE THE HOUSE TO MYSELF...
GO TRAVELLING... GET FIT...
RESTART MY CAREER..."

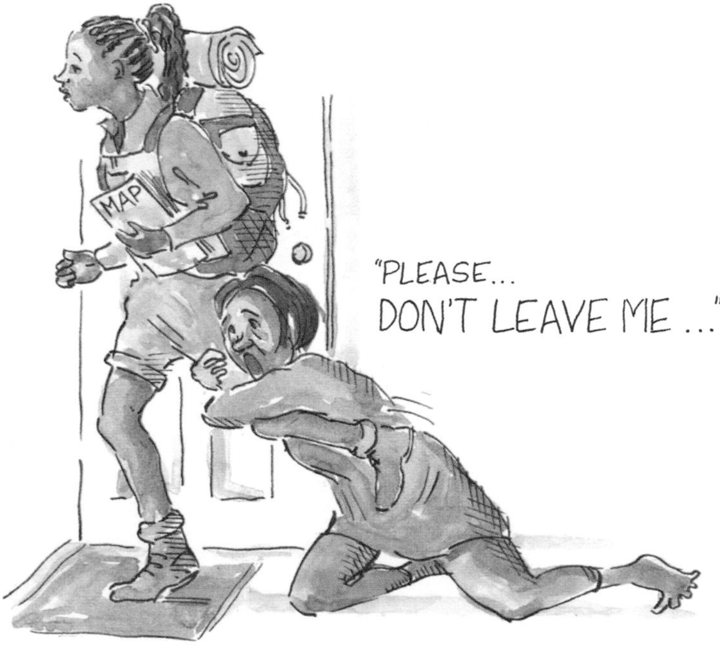
MAP
"PLEASE...
DON'T LEAVE ME ..."

PARENT (tiger mum)

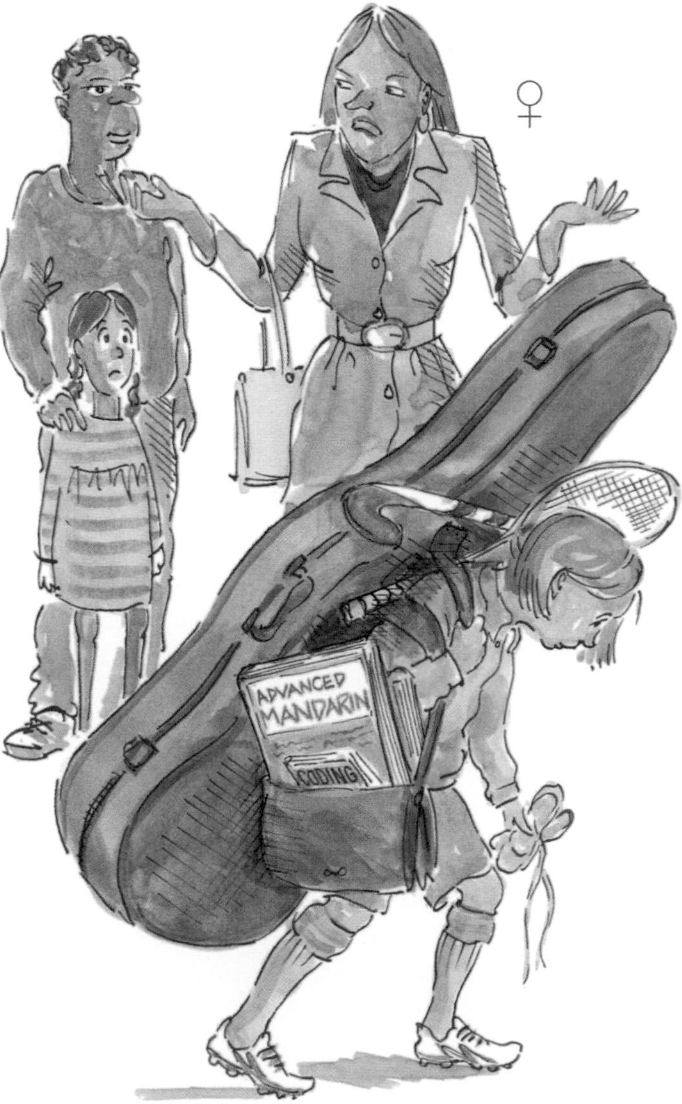
♀
ADVANCED MANDARIN
CODING

VICAR (traditional)

holy

♂

Observing a Vicar (traditional) through the seasons:

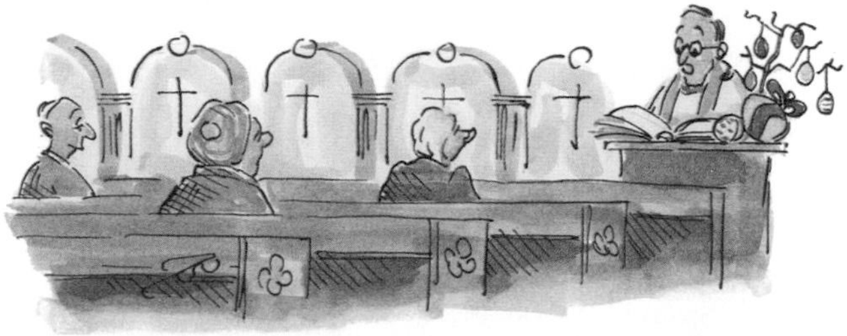

Spring

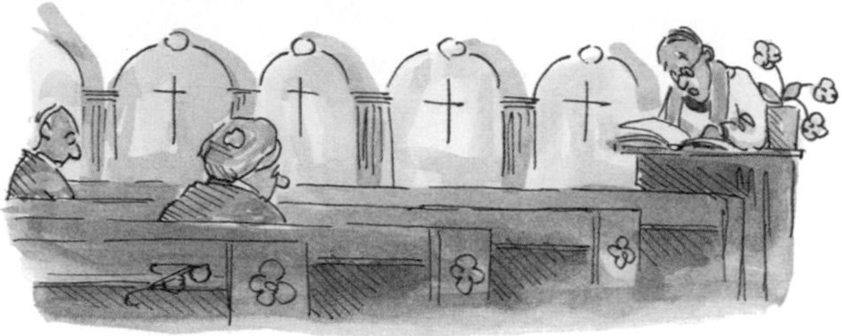

Summer

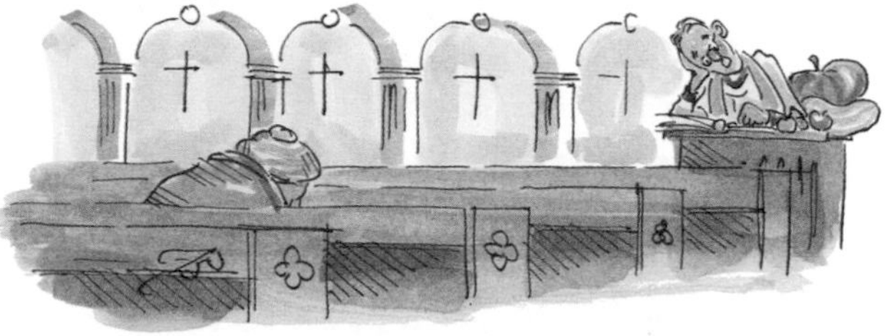

Autumn

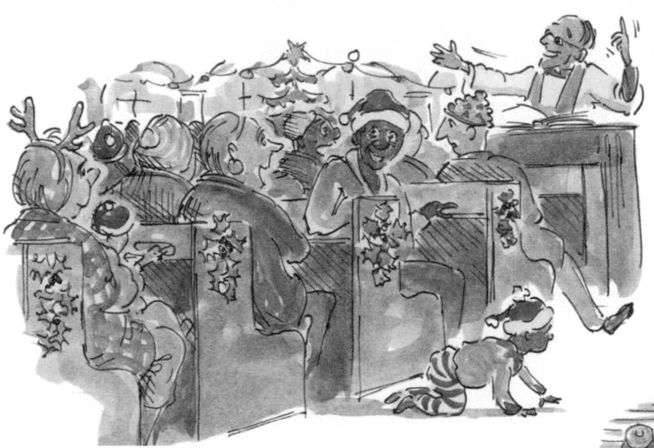

Christmas

Staple diet:

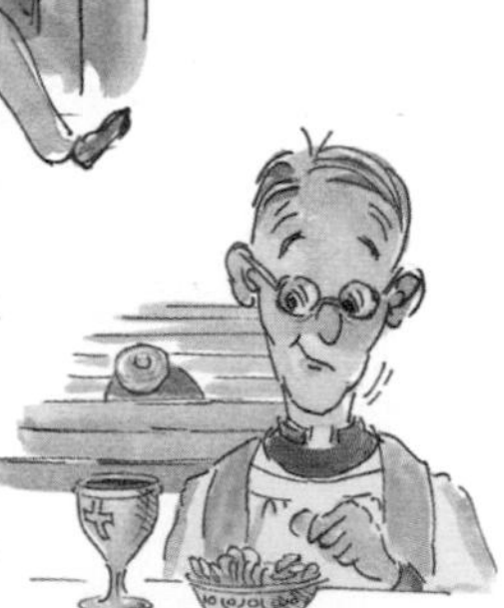

FOODIE

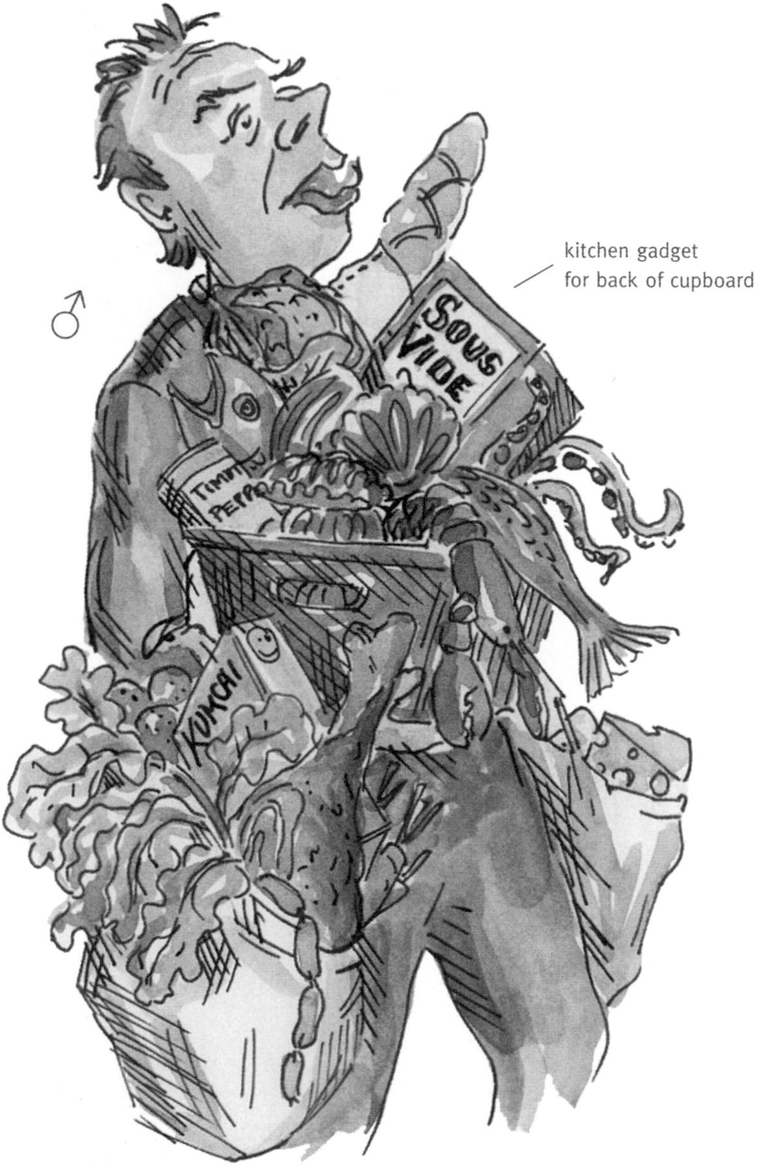
kitchen gadget
for back of cupboard
SOUS
VIDE
♂

Behaviour (repetitive):

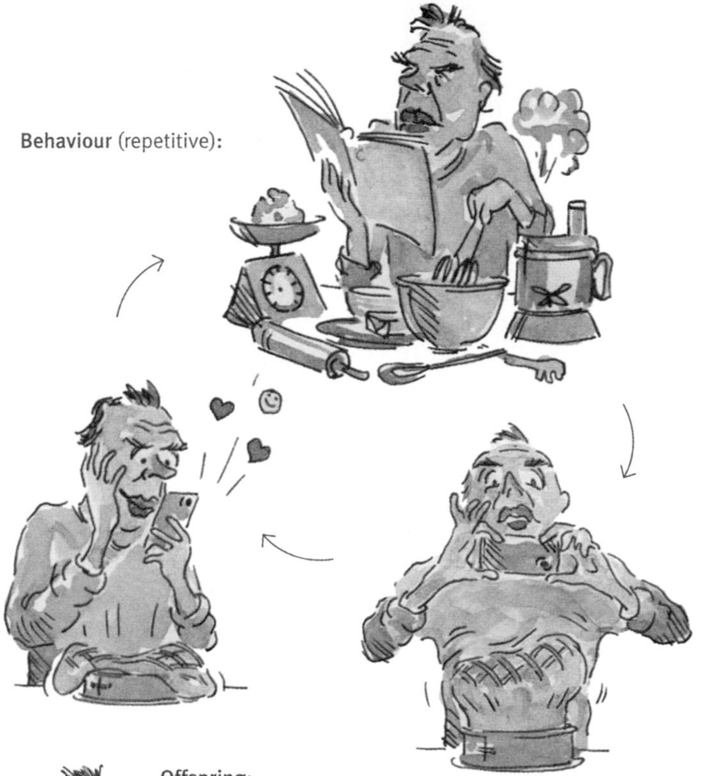

Offspring:

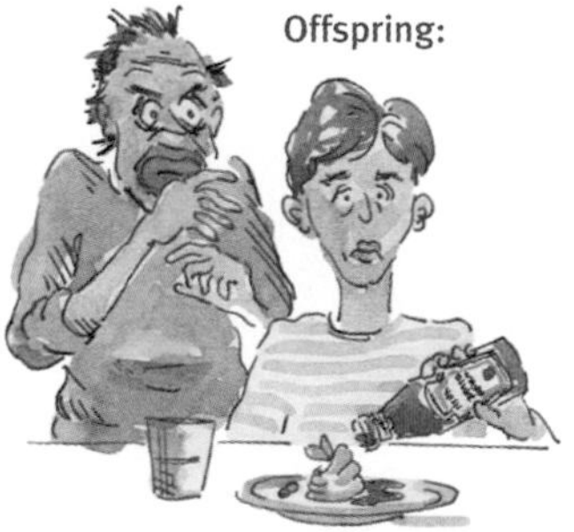

Distribution:

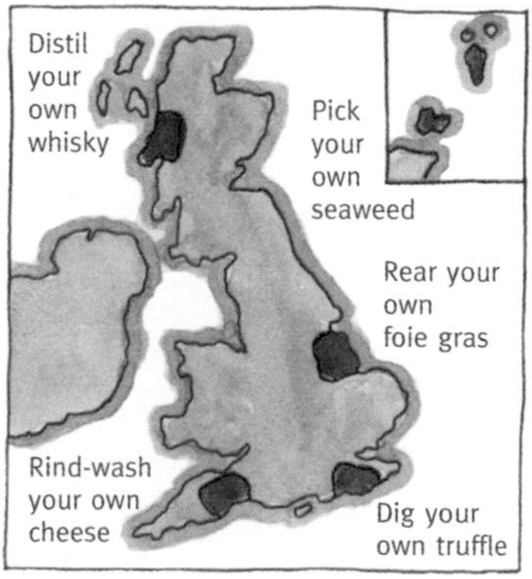
Distil your own whisky
Pick your own seaweed
Rear your own foie gras
Rind-wash your own cheese
Dig your own truffle

Mate:

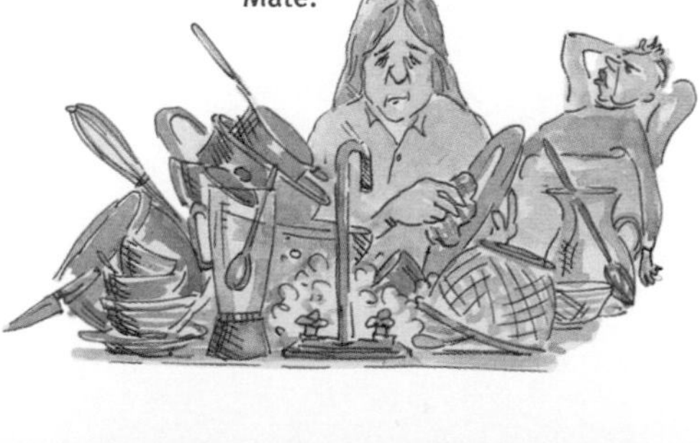

IDENTIFICATION CHART
(widespread)

Profile	Tracks	Species
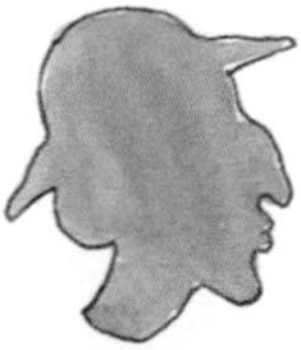	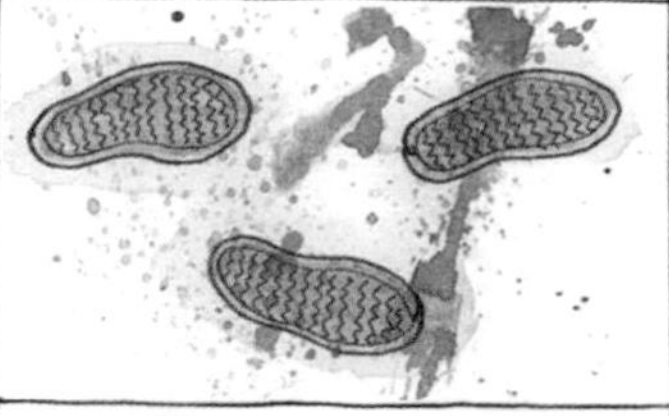	Artist
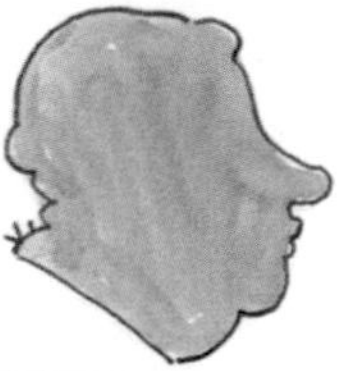	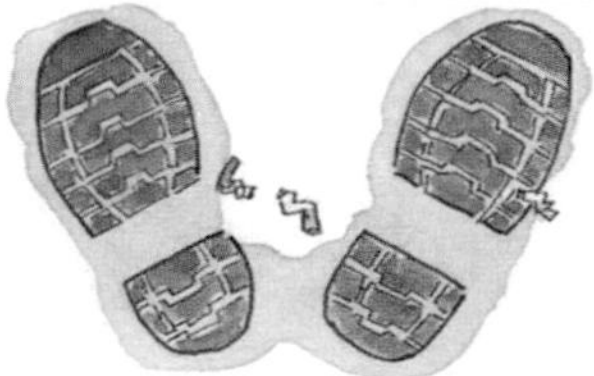	Builder (traditional)
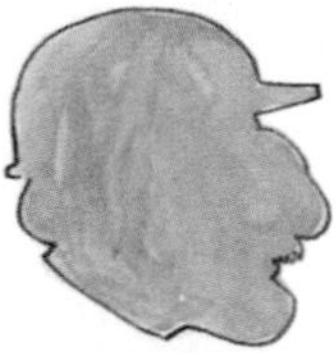	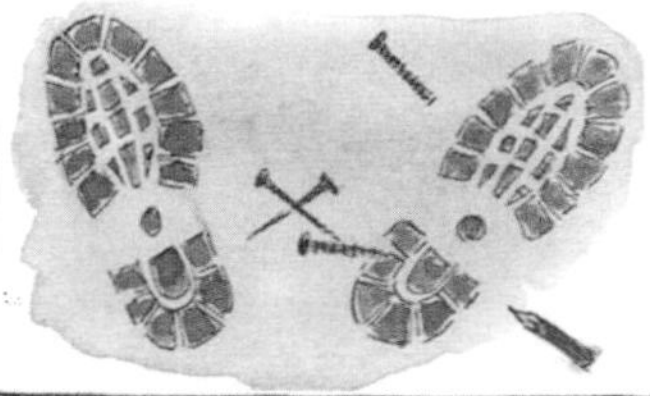	Builder (Polish)
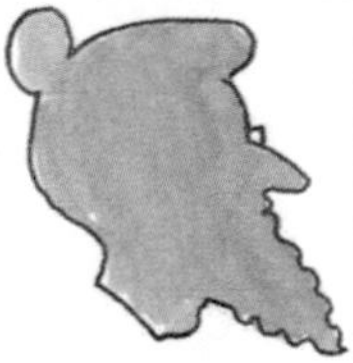	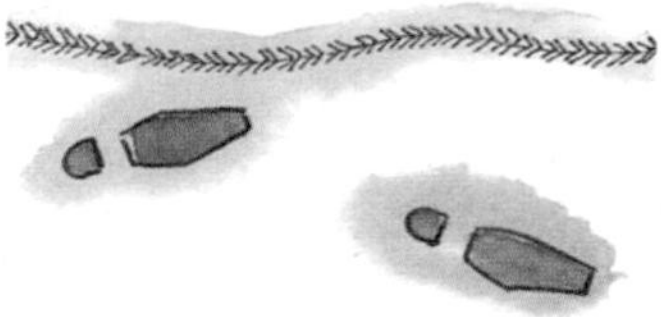	Hipster
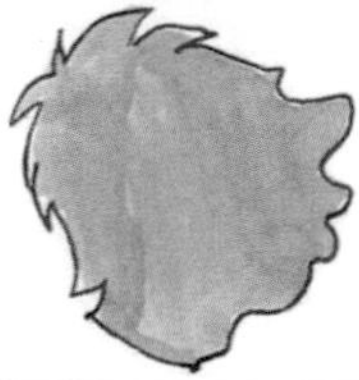	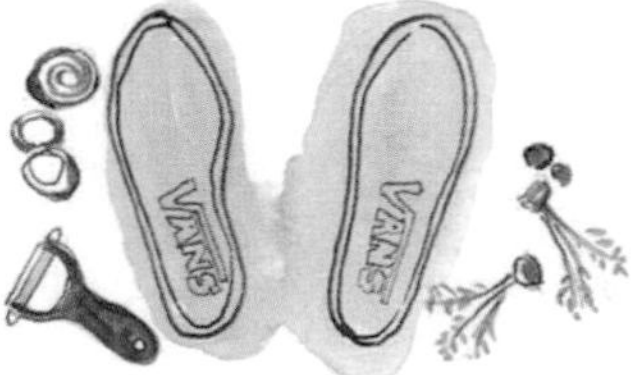 VANS VANS	Foodie

	Parent (yummy mummy)
	Hairstylist
VEGAN	Therapist
	Parent (single mum)
	Local Councillor
	Parent (single dad)

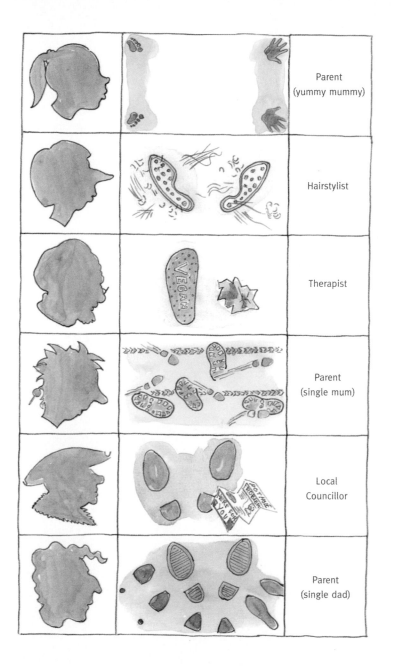

SURFER / YACHTIE / HOLIDAYMAKER
OPERA LOVER / FESTIVALGOER
FOREST SCHOOL LEADER / NATURE WRITER (seasonal)

SURFER

♂

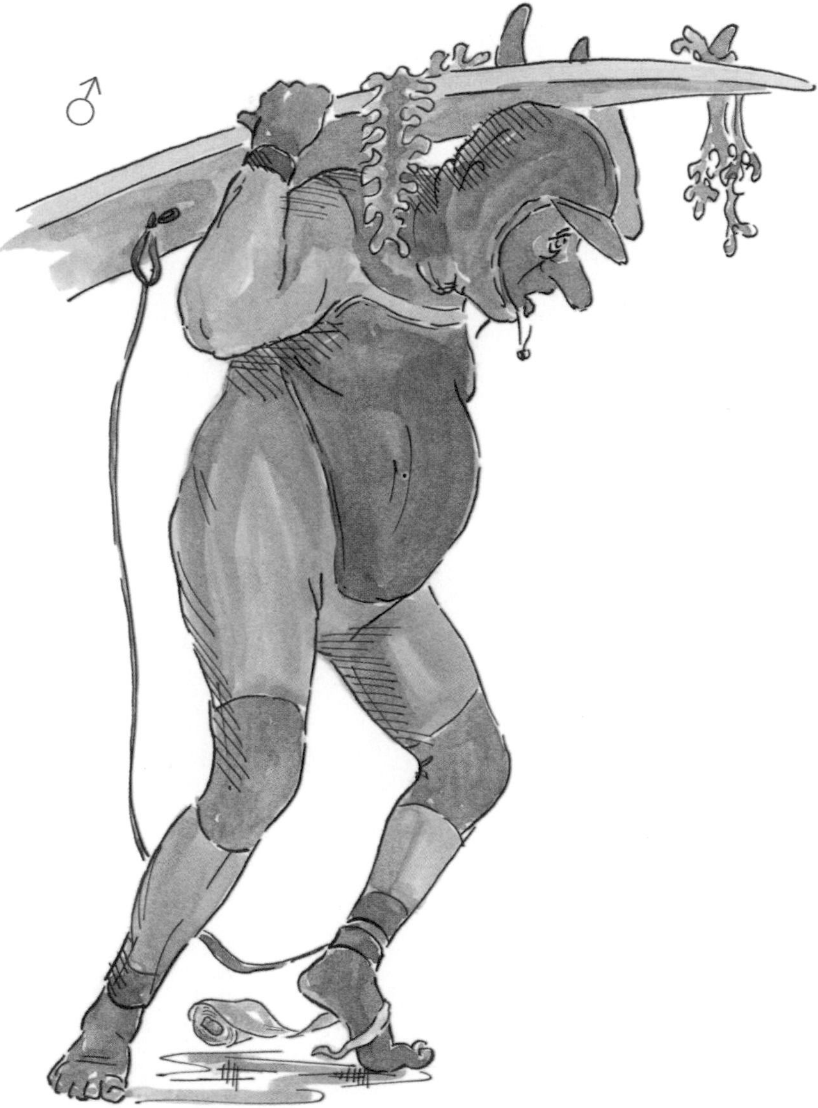

Mating display:

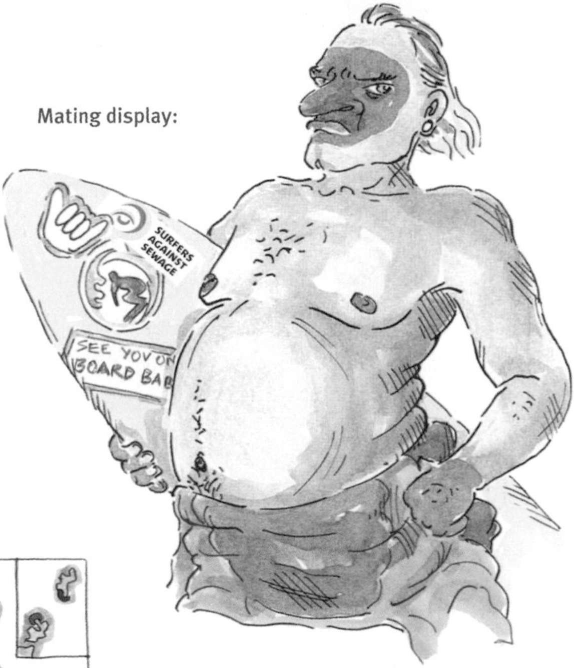
SURFERS AGAINST SEWAGE

Distribution:

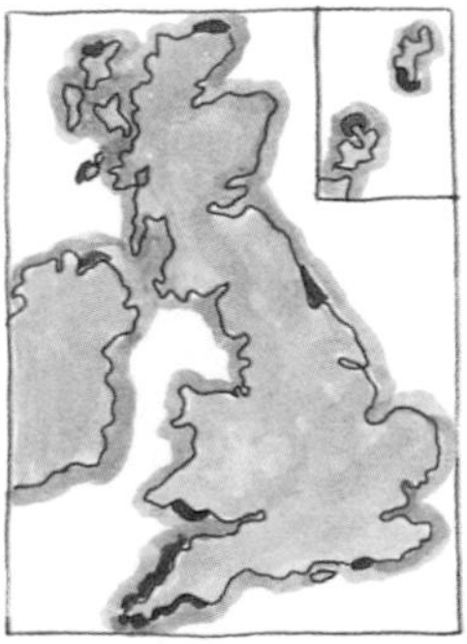

Habitat:

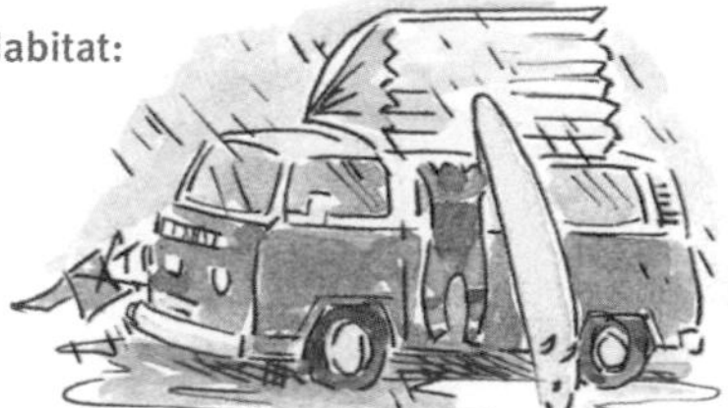

Observing a Surfer through the day:*

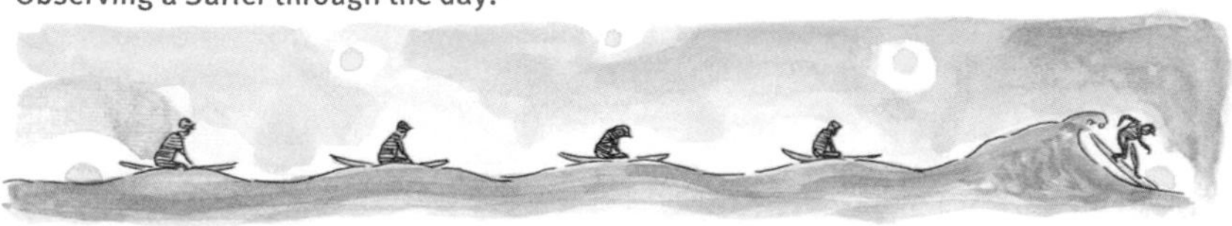

*not to be confused with a Paraglider, an airbound species

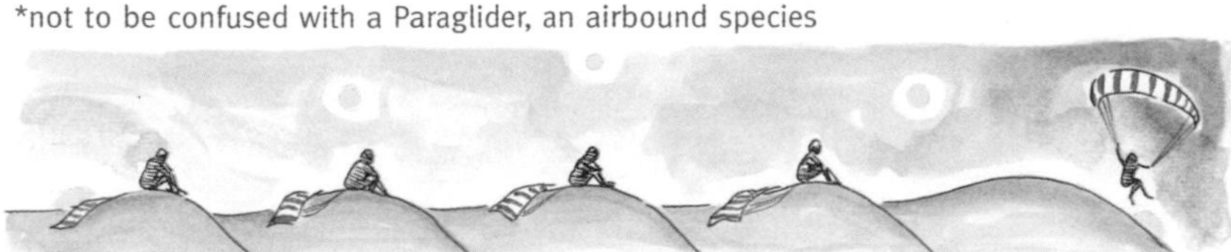

YACHTIE

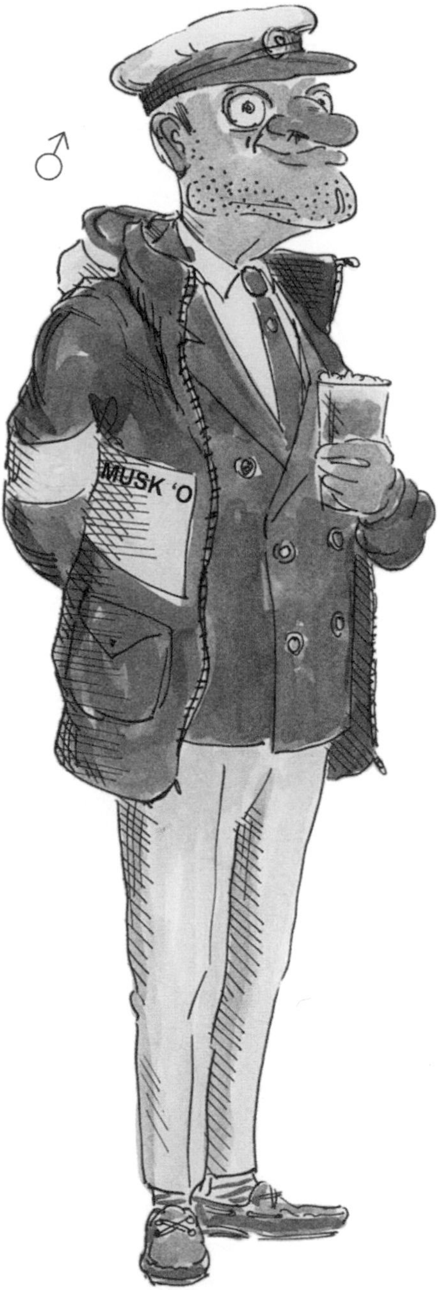
♂
MUSK 'O

Mating display:

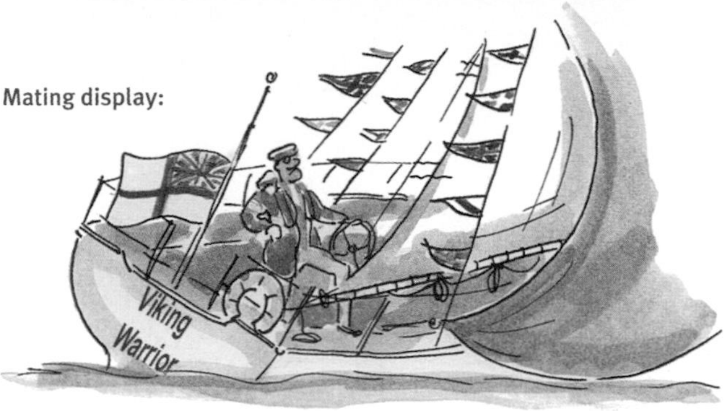
Viking
Warrior

Interaction with other species:

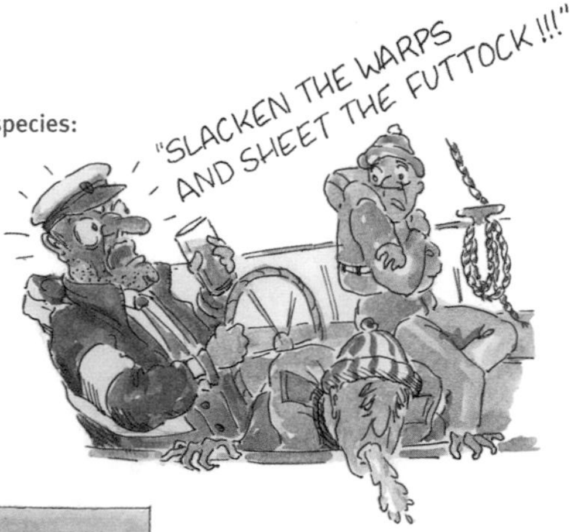
"SLACKEN THE WARPS
AND SHEET THE FUTTOCK !!!"

Distribution:

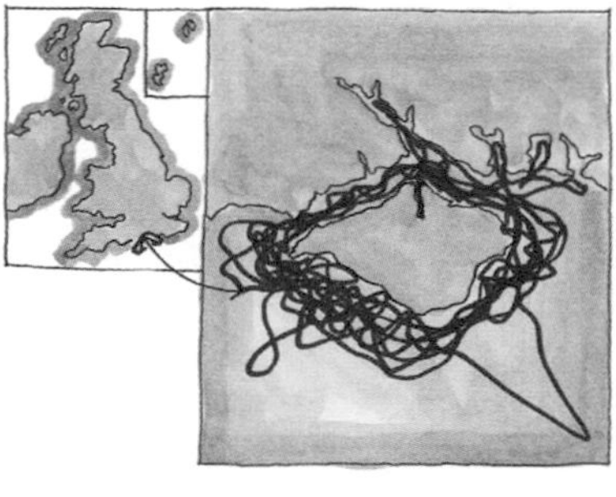

Isle of Wight

Habitat:

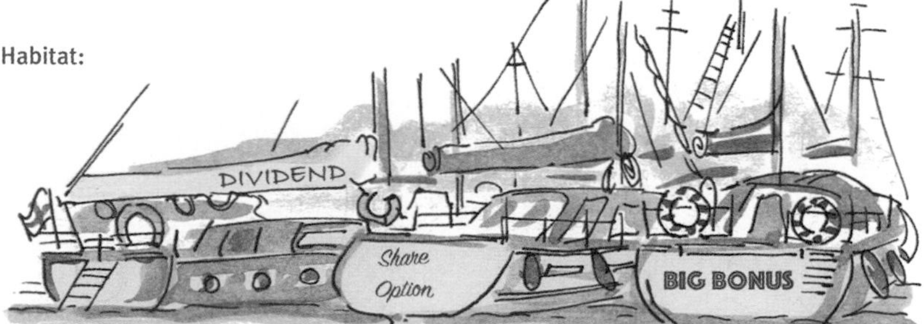
DIVIDEND
Share
Option
BIG BONUS

HOLIDAYMAKER (package)

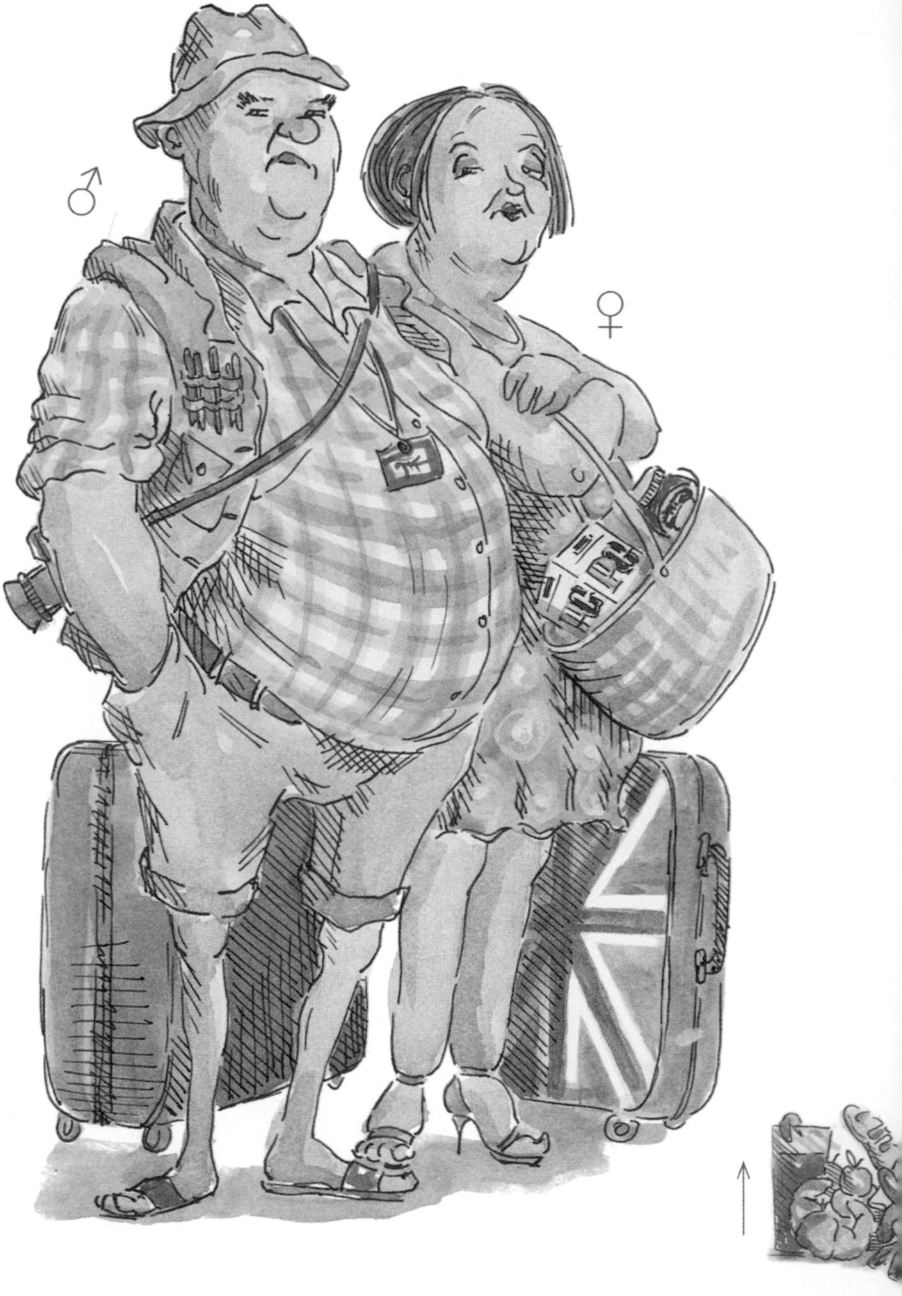

Habitat:

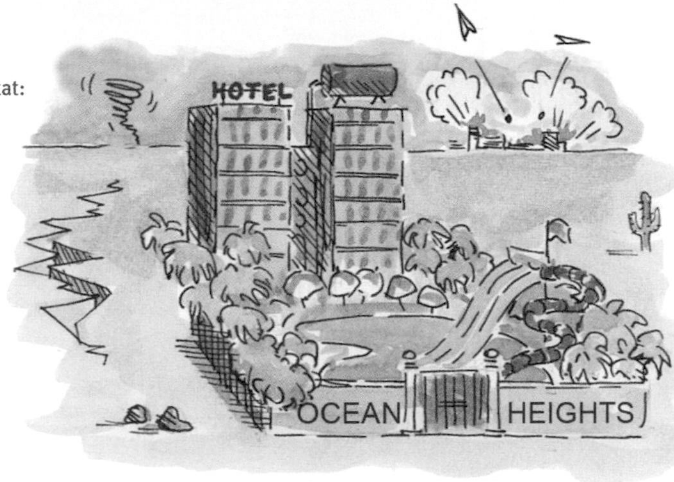
HOTEL
OCEAN
HEIGHTS

Behaviour:

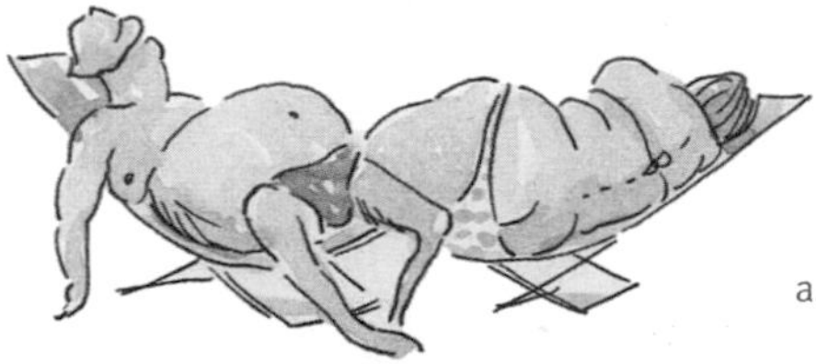

a.m.

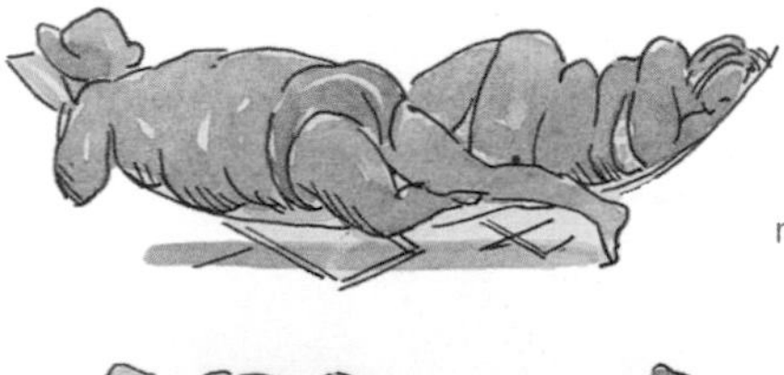

midday

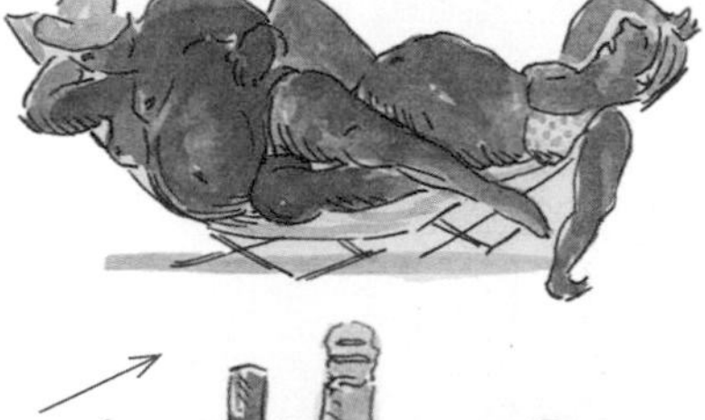

p.m.

Migratory route:

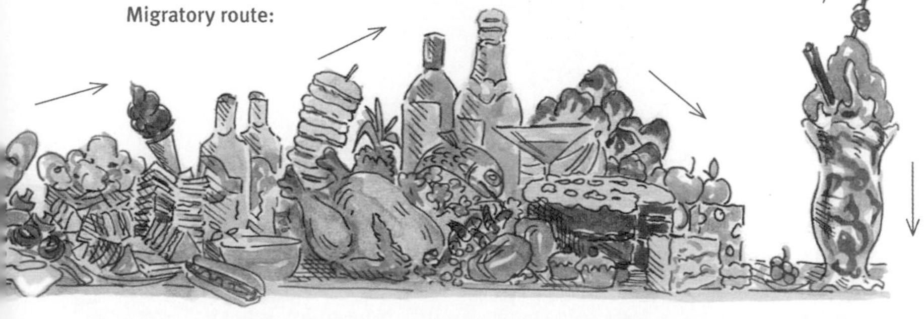

OPERA LOVER

♂

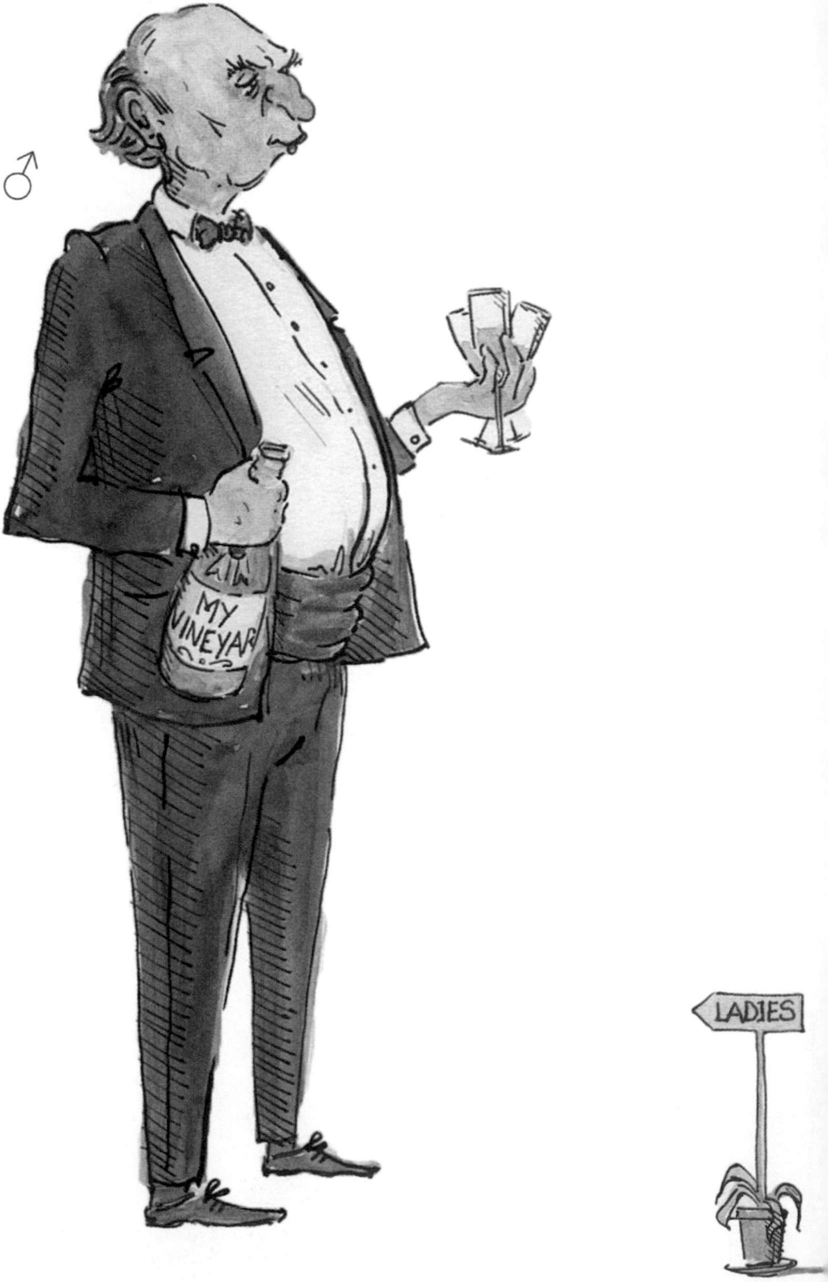

MY VINEYAR
LADIES

Primary facial expressions:

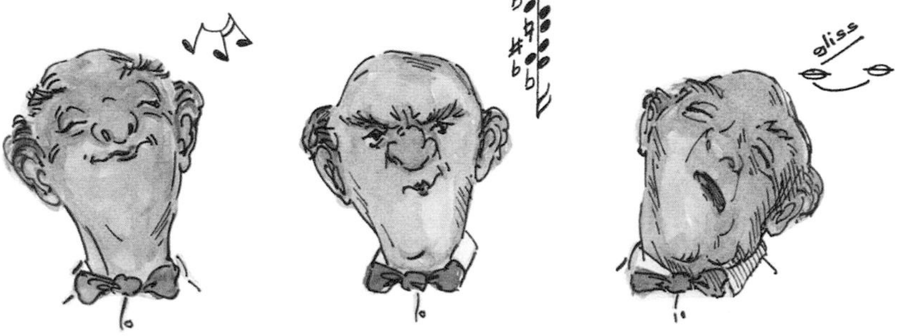
gliss

ecstatic challenged content

Plumage:

♀

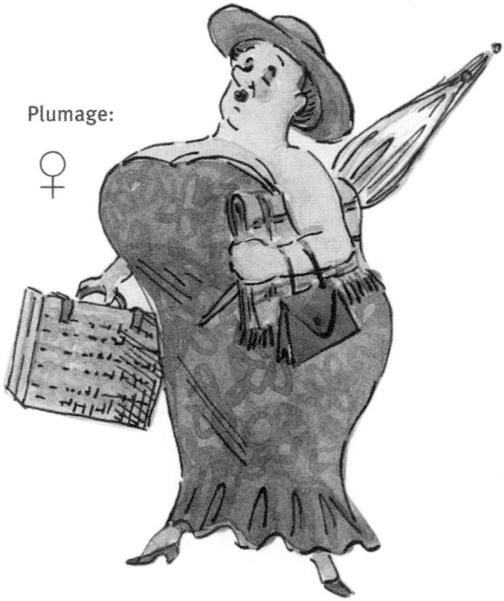

Staple diet: salmon

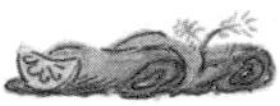

smoked

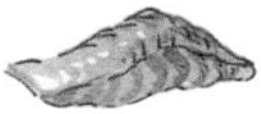

poached

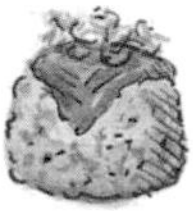

mousse

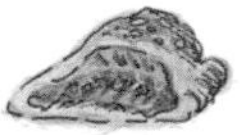

en croute

Flocking in same-sex groups:

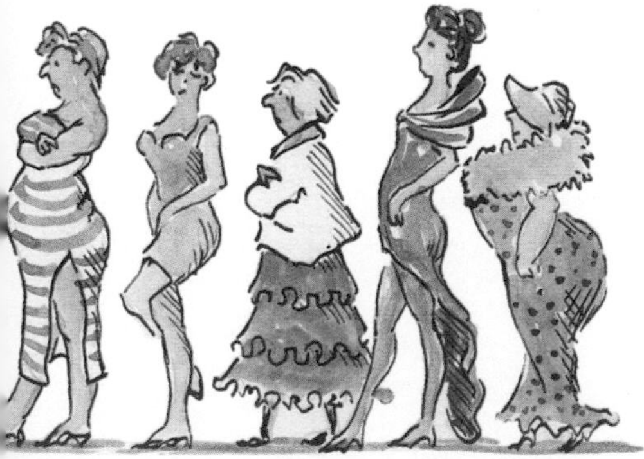

Distribution:

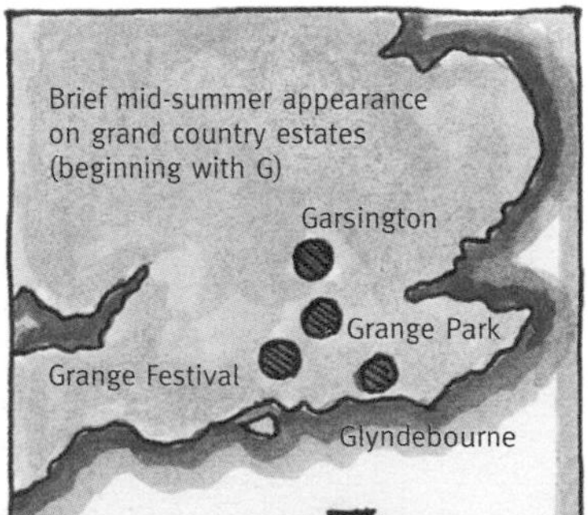
Brief mid-summer appearance
on grand country estates
(beginning with G)
Garsington
Grange Park
Grange Festival
Glyndebourne
here

FESTIVALGOER
(middle class)

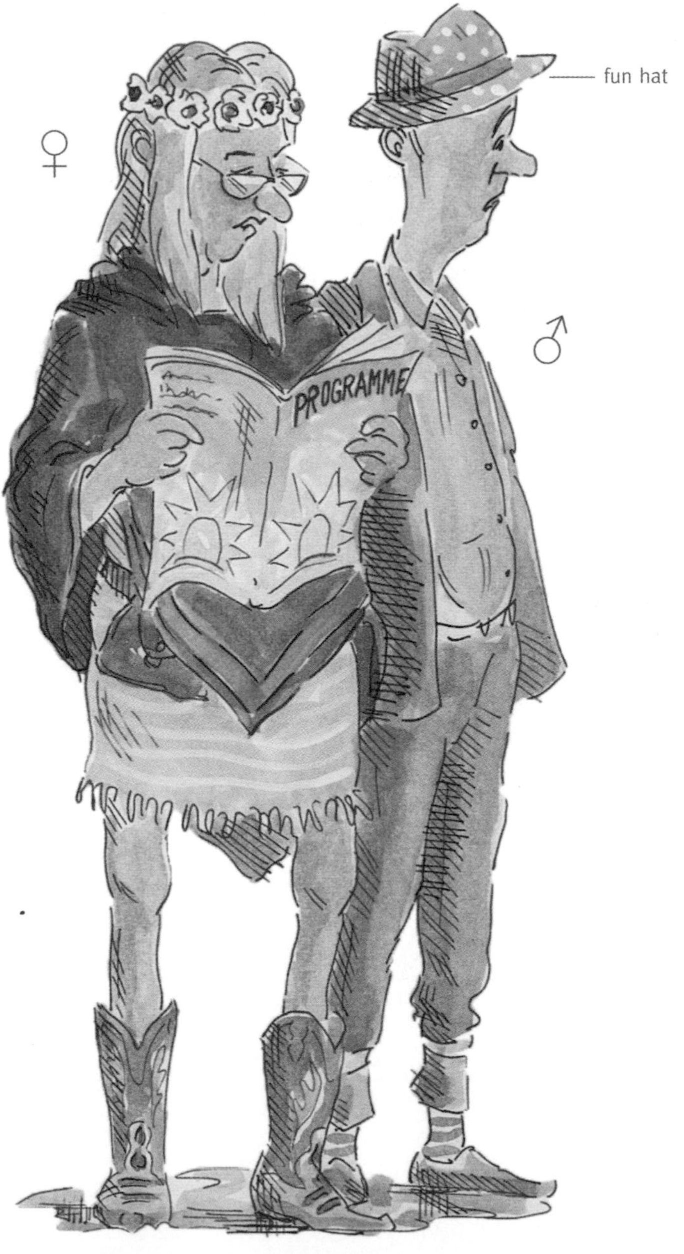
fun hat
♀
♂
PROGRAMME

Observing a Festivalgoer (middle class) in the field:

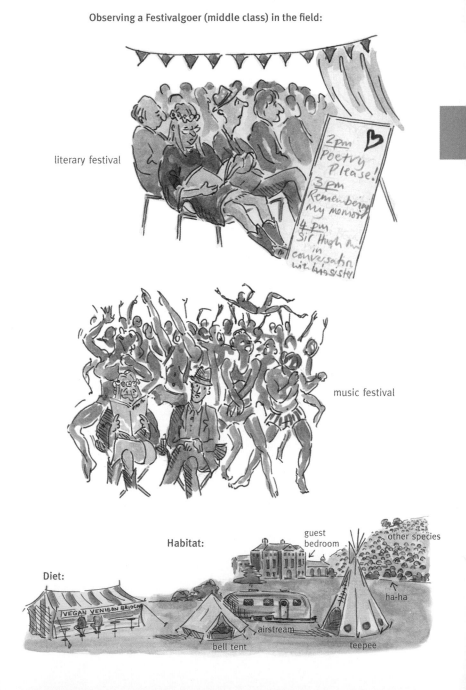

literary festival

2pm
Poetry
Please! ♥
3pm
Remembering
my memoir
4pm
Sir Hugh —
in
conversation
with his sister

music festival

Habitat:

Diet:

guest
bedroom

other species

VEGAN VENISON BURGER

bell tent

airstream

teepee

ha-ha

FOREST SCHOOL LEADER

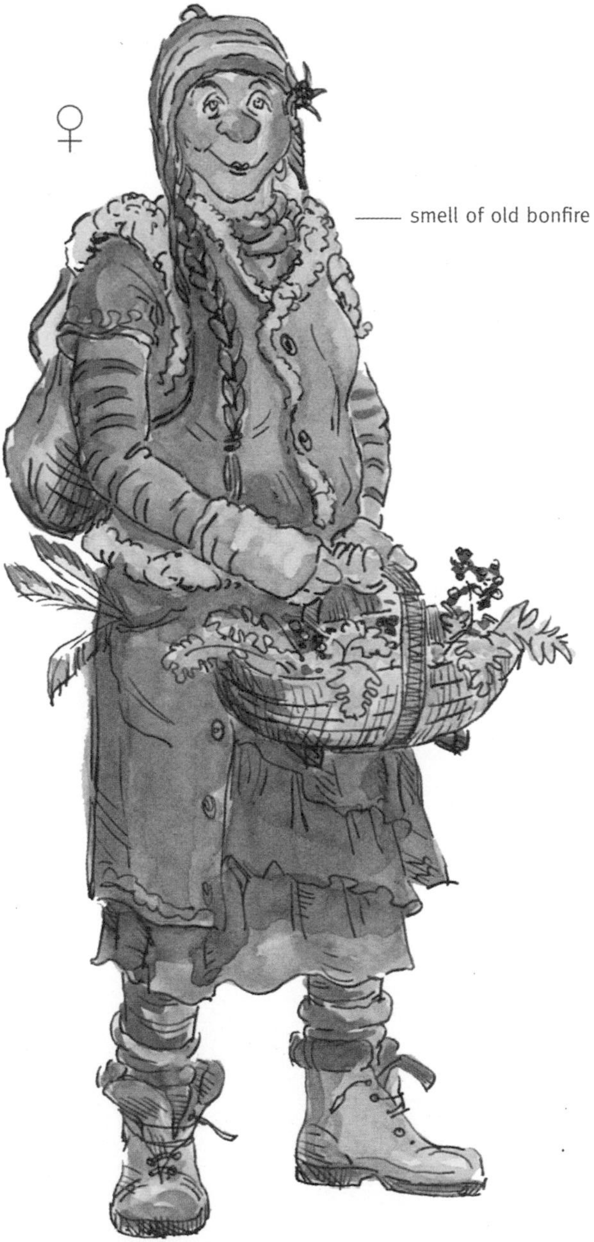
♀
smell of old bonfire

Tracking a Forest School Leader in the wild:

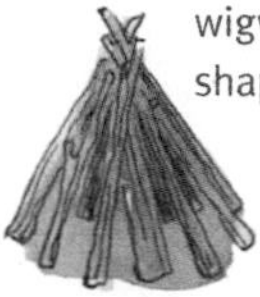

wigwam shapes

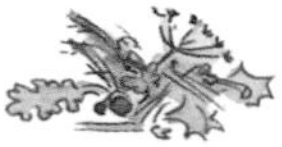

tinder

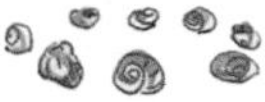

circles of shells, stones, etc.

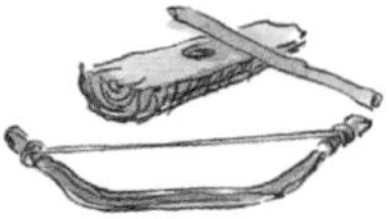

firebow

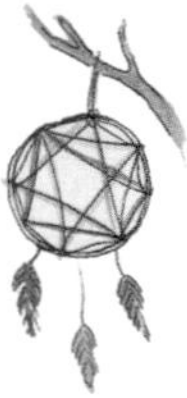

dreamcatcher

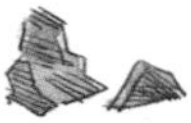

flints

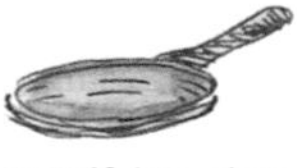

magnifying glass

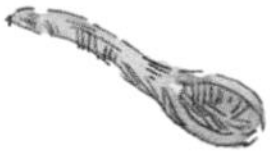

whittled objects

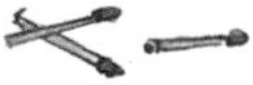

matches

Plumage:

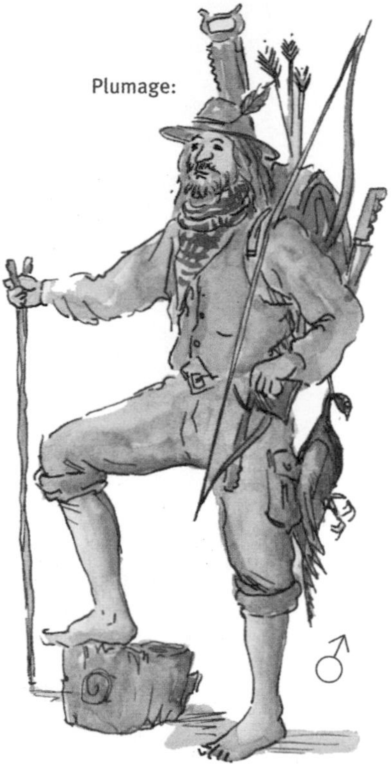
♂

Habitat:

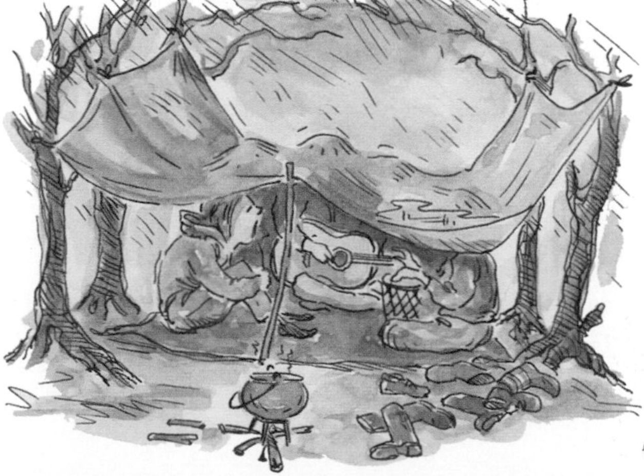

Staple diet:

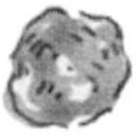

dough balls

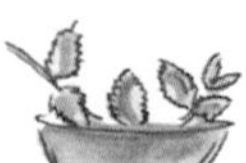

nettle soup

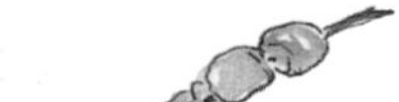

marshmallows

NATURE WRITER

skylark

♂

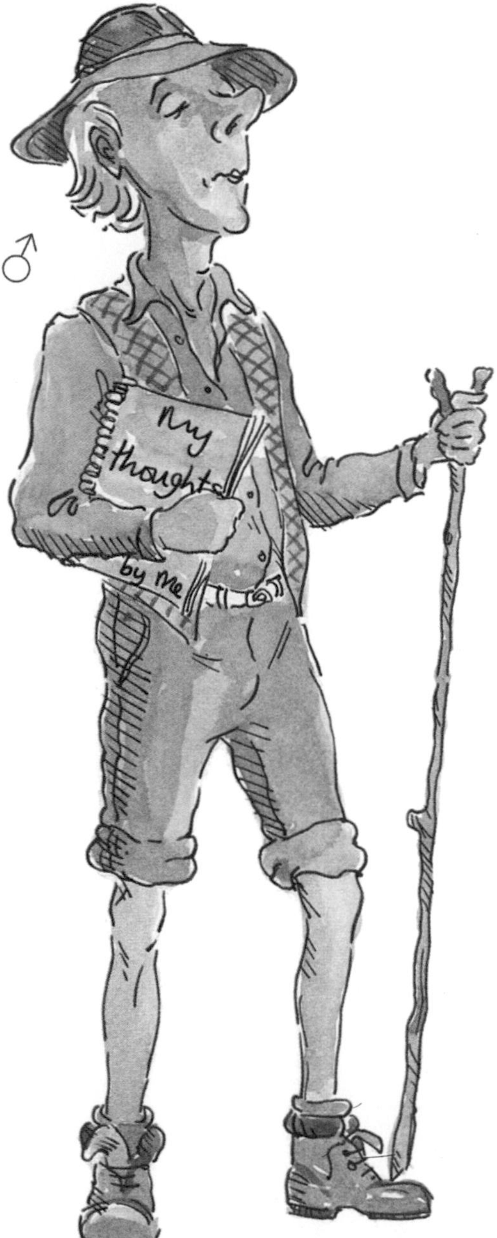
My thoughts
by me

Spoor:

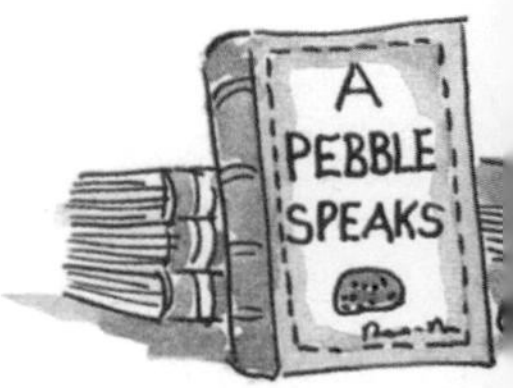
A PEBBLE SPEAKS

Behaviour:

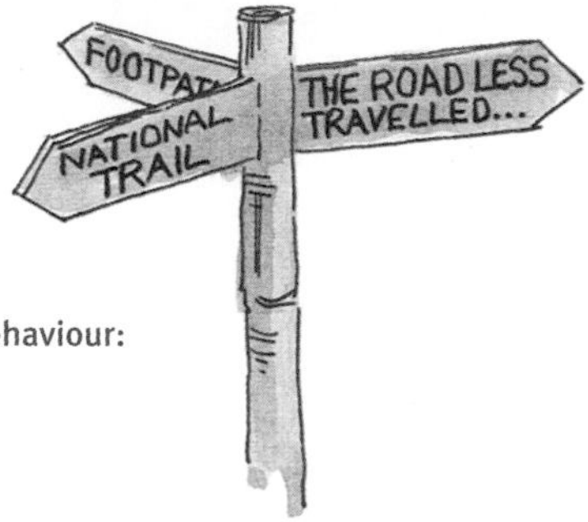
FOOTPAT
NATIONAL TRAIL
THE ROAD LESS TRAVELLED...

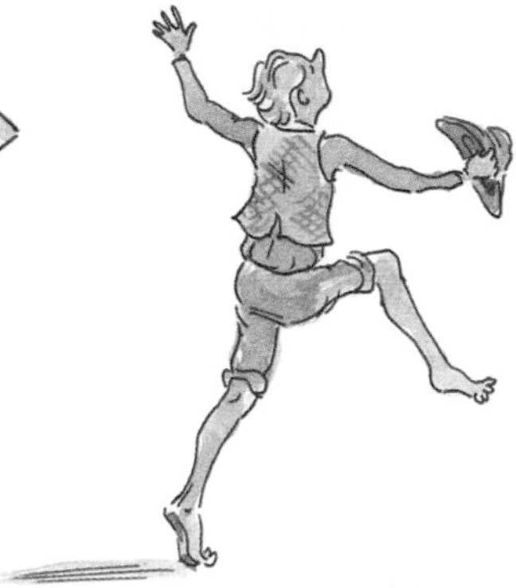

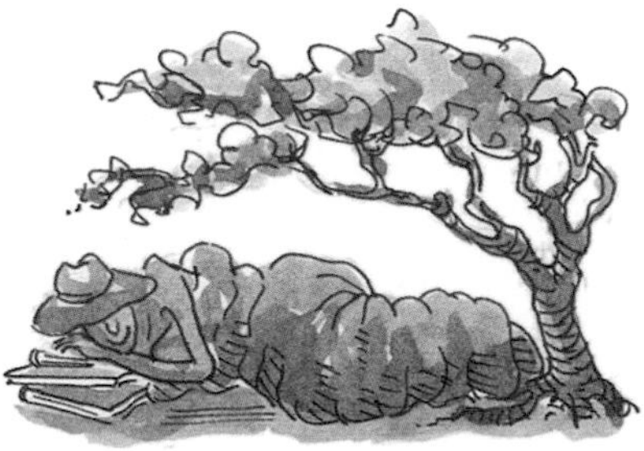

sleeping out

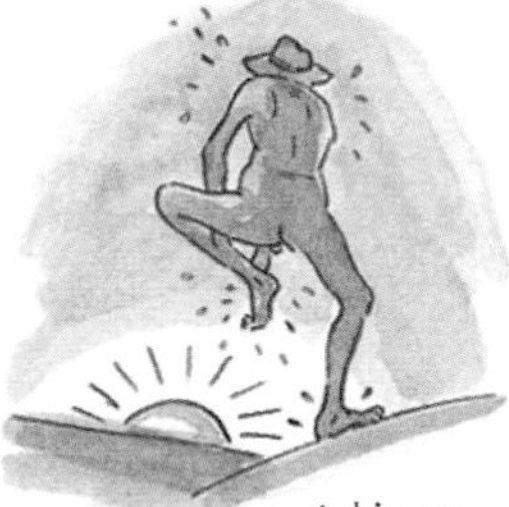

taking a dew bath

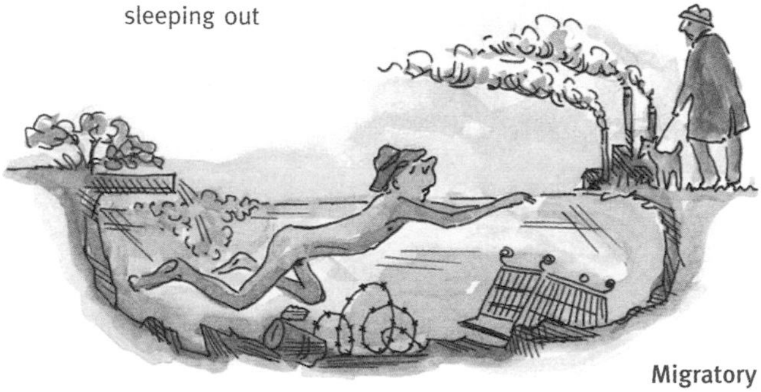

wild swimming

Migratory routes:

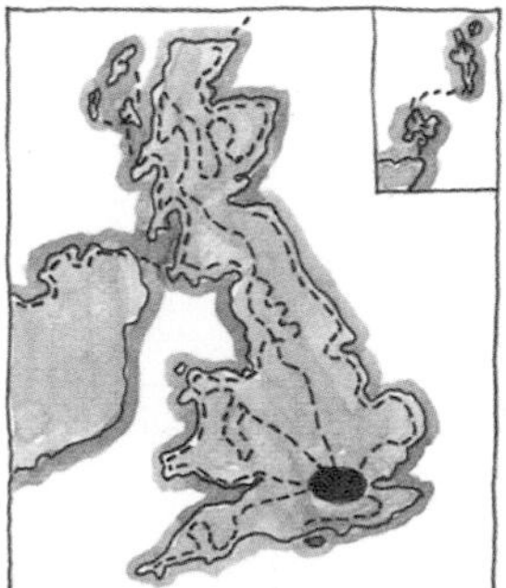

Book launches

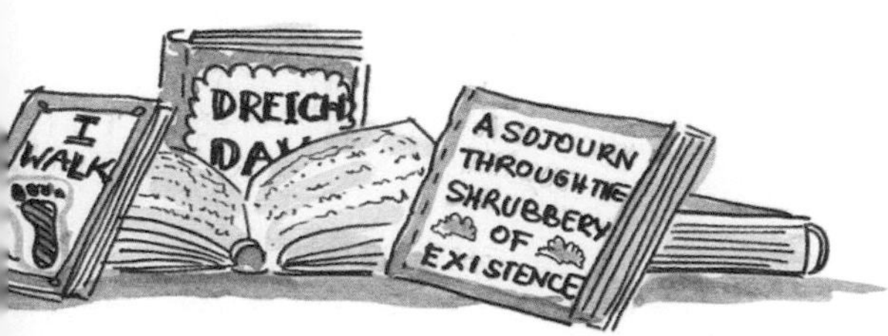
I WALK
DREICH
A SOJOURN THROUGH THE SHRUBBERY OF EXISTENCE

IDENTIFICATION CHART
(seasonal)

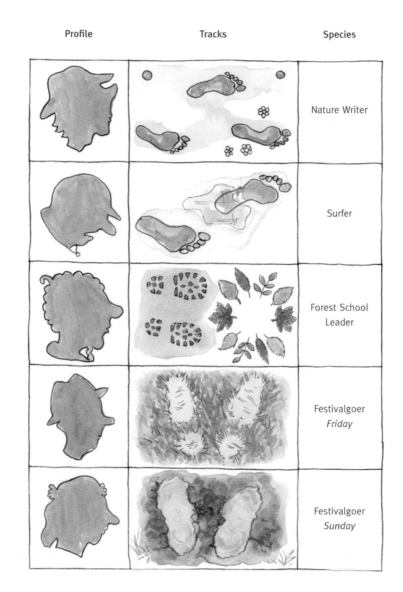

Profile	Tracks	Species
		Nature Writer
		Surfer
		Forest School Leader
		Festivalgoer *Friday*
		Festivalgoer *Sunday*

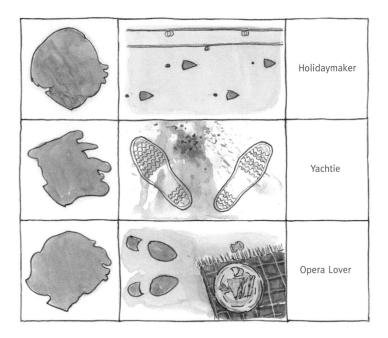

		Holidaymaker
		Yachtie
		Opera Lover

Seasonal distribution:

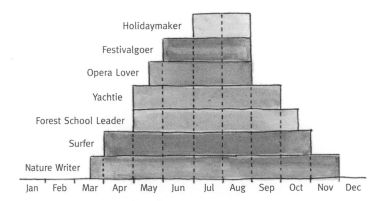

Holidaymaker
Festivalgoer
Opera Lover
Yachtie
Forest School Leader
Surfer
Nature Writer

Jan · Feb · Mar · Apr · May · Jun · Jul · Aug · Sep · Oct · Nov · Dec

YOUTH / TRUSTAFARIAN / STUDENT / PUPIL (juveniles)

YOUTH

♂

designer brand

Marking territory:

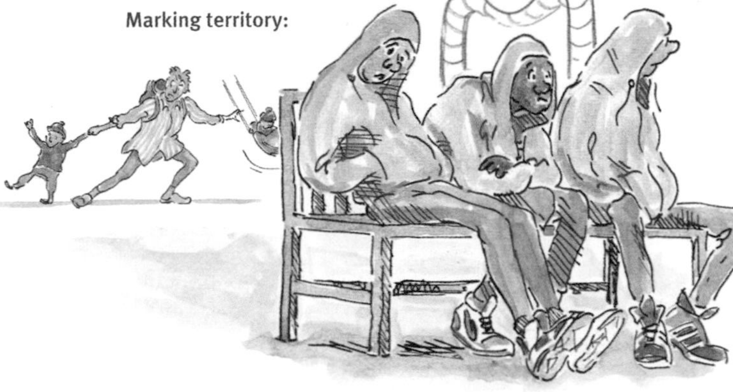

Signalling:

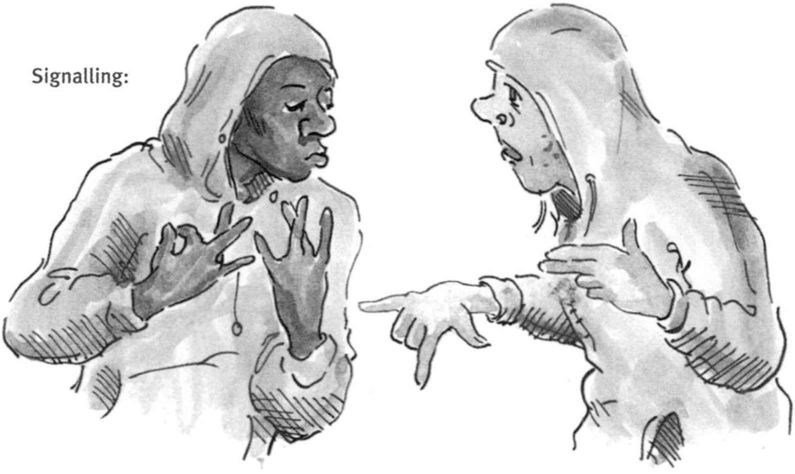

Staple diet:

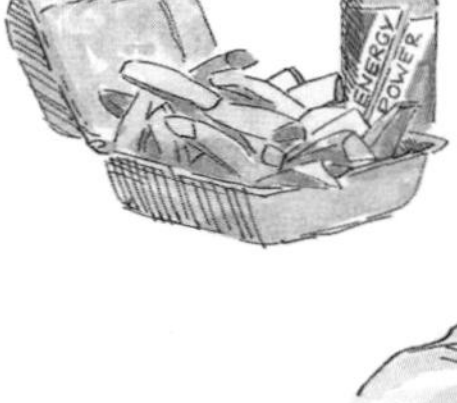
ENERGY POWER

Nest:

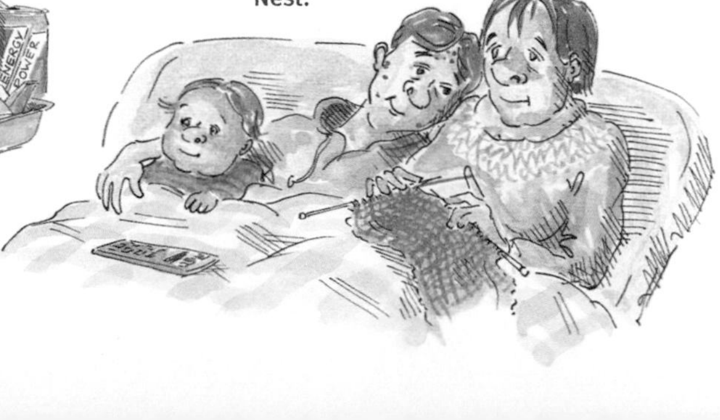

TRUSTAFARIAN

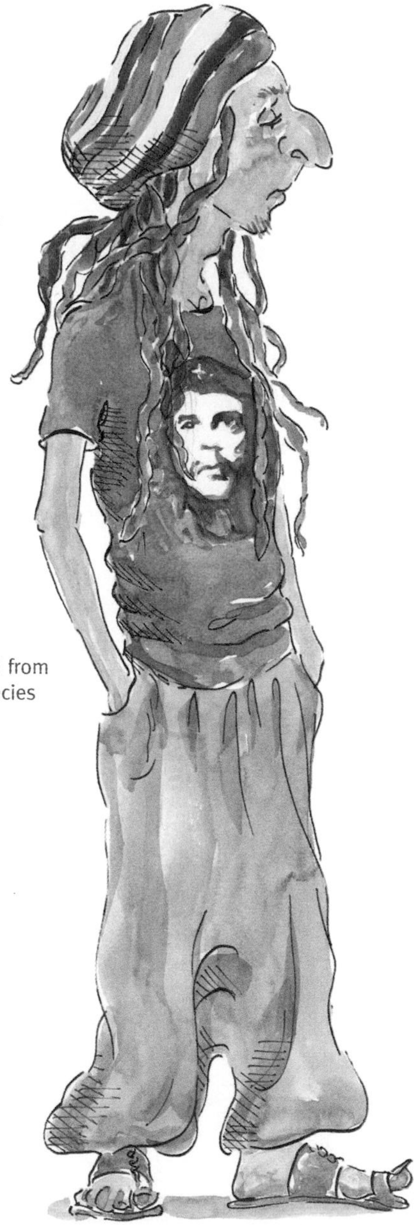
♂
plumage
borrowed from
other species

Staple diet:

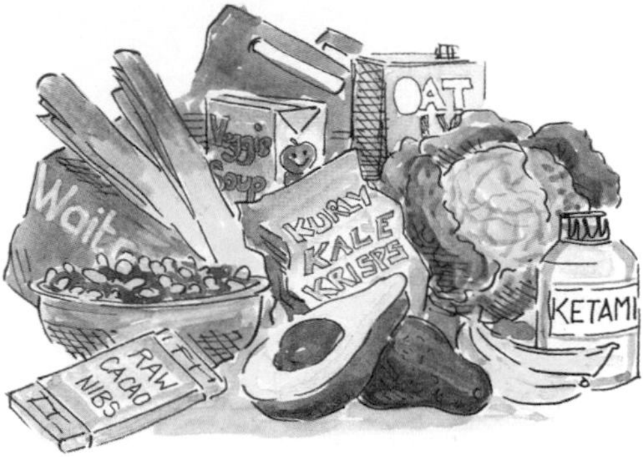
OAT
Veggie Soup
KURLY KALE KRISPS
KETAMI
RAW CACAO NIBS

Behaviour:

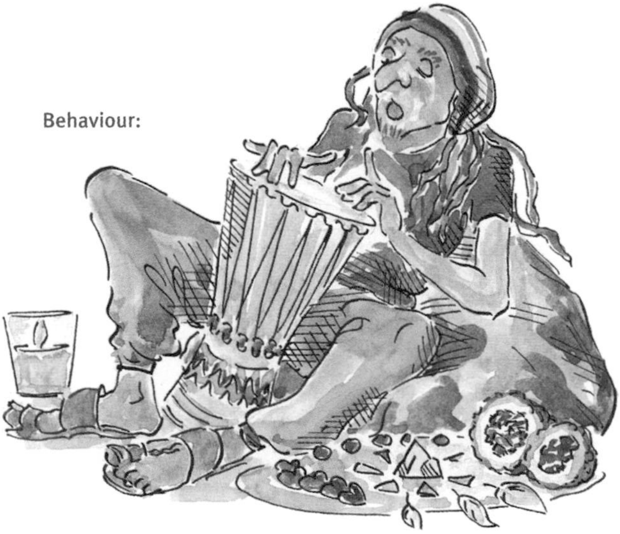

Nest:

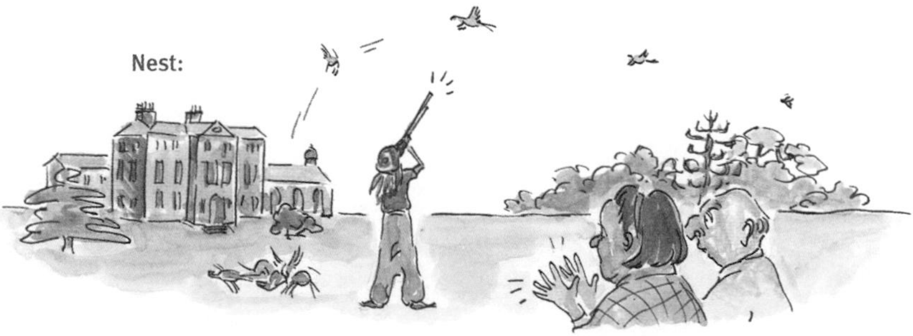

STUDENT (gap year)

ORPHANAGES OF SOUTH AMERICA
♀
dioralyte
SAVE

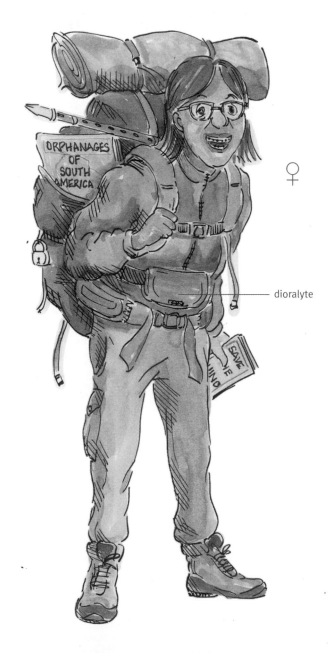

Observing a Student (gap year) on departure and return:

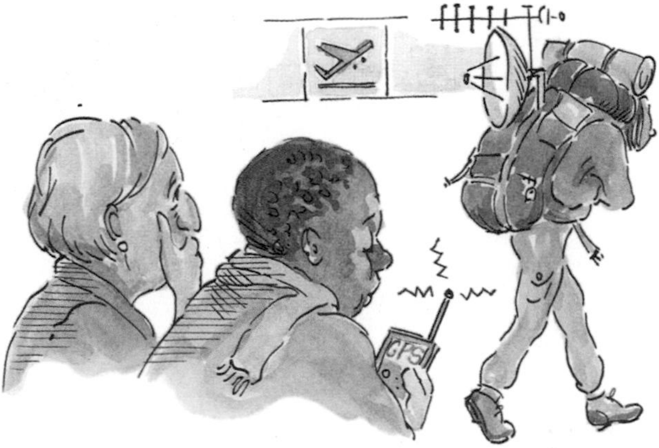
GPS

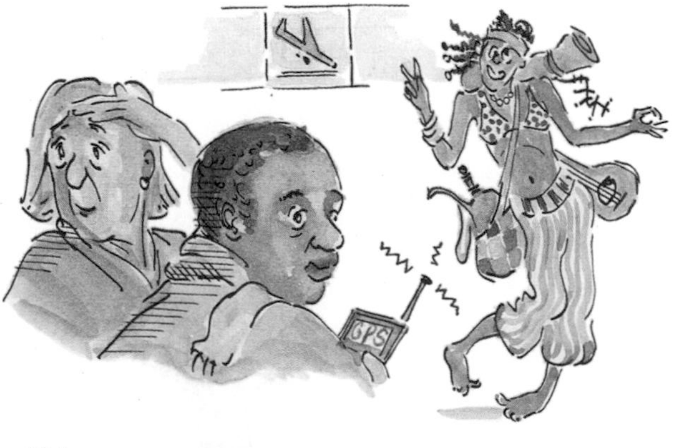
GPS

Diet:

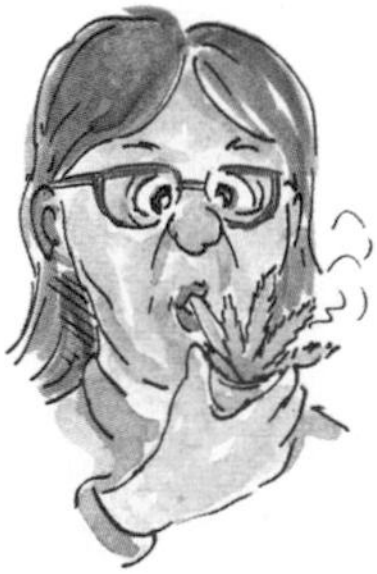

marijuana

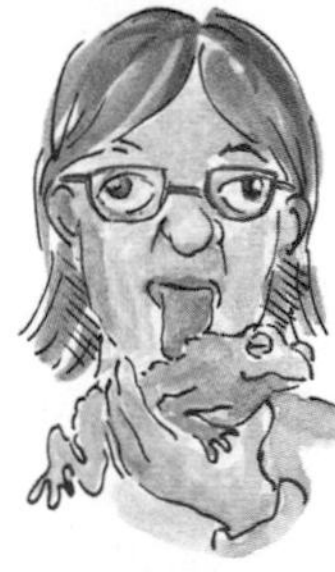

hallucinogenic toad

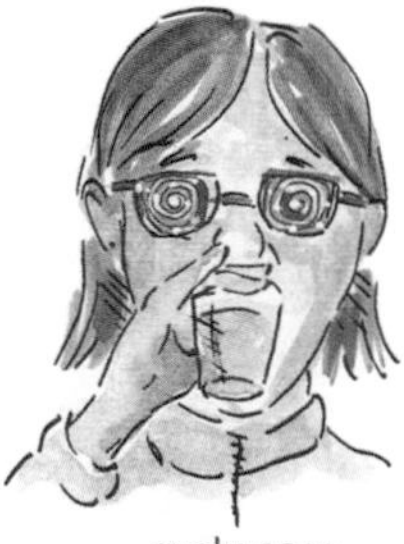

ayahuasca

PUPIL (primary)

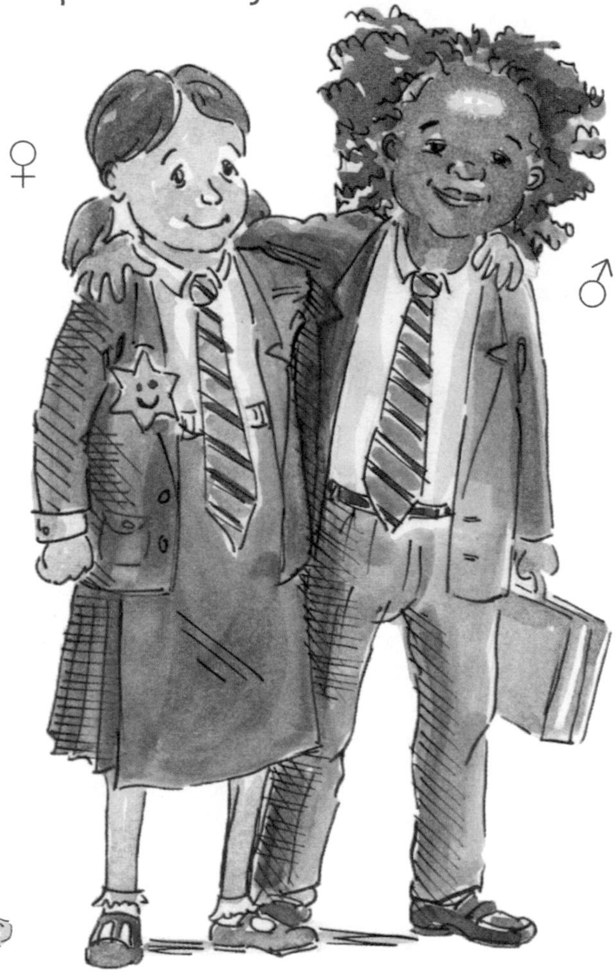
♀
♂

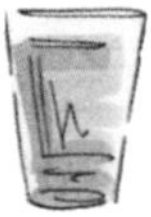

Staple diet:

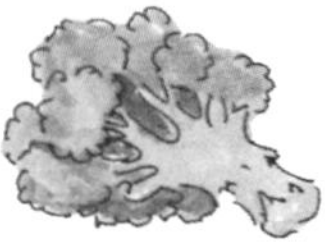

Habitat:

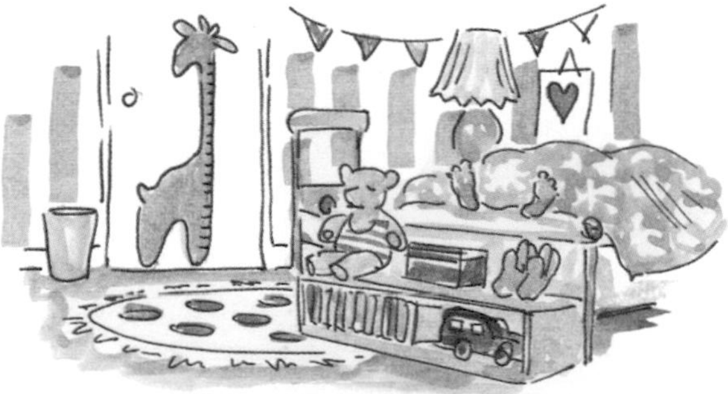

(secondary)

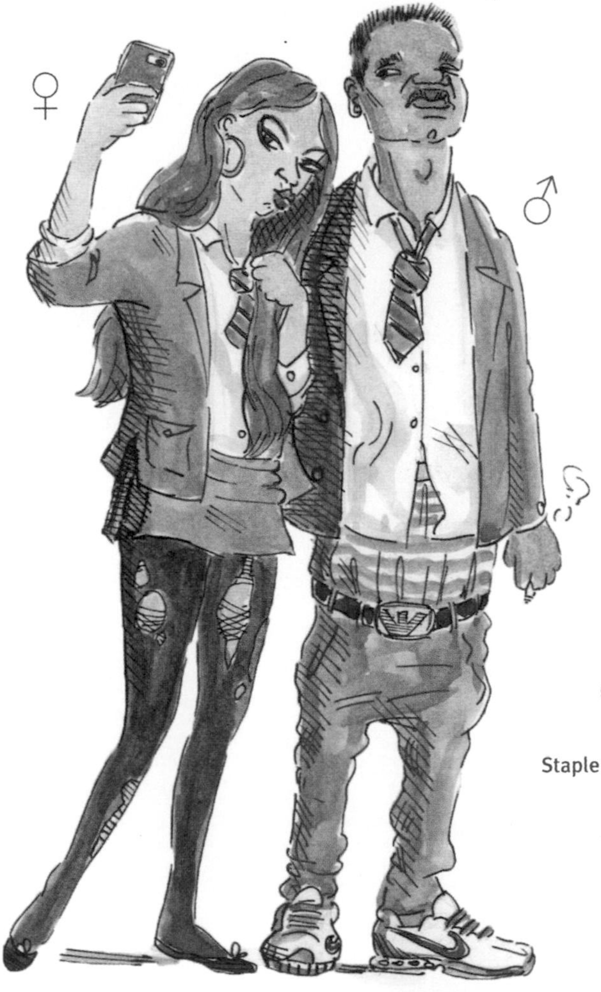

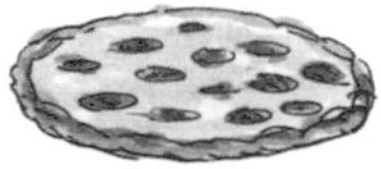

Staple diet:

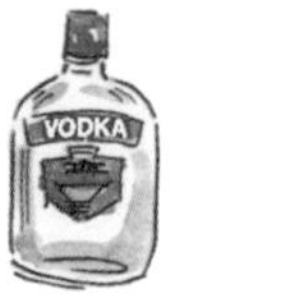
VODKA

Habitat:

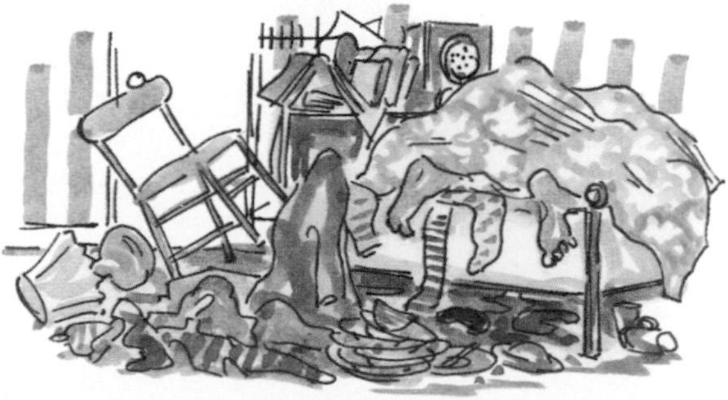

PUPIL (home-schooled)

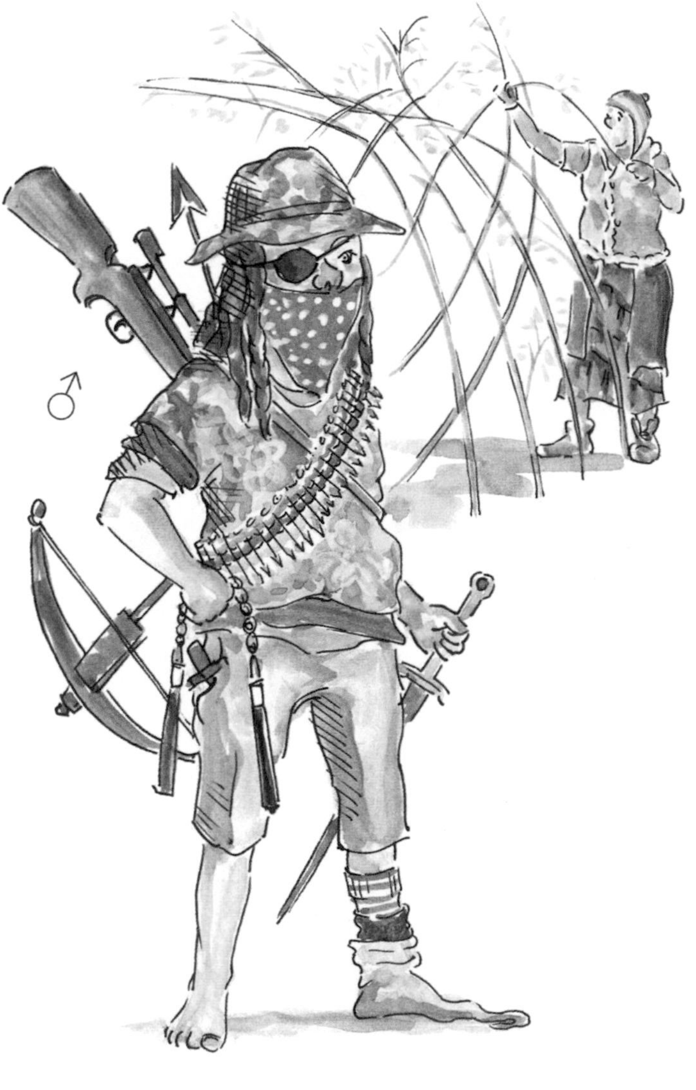

PUPIL (boarder)

PUPIL (year 10*)

Teacher

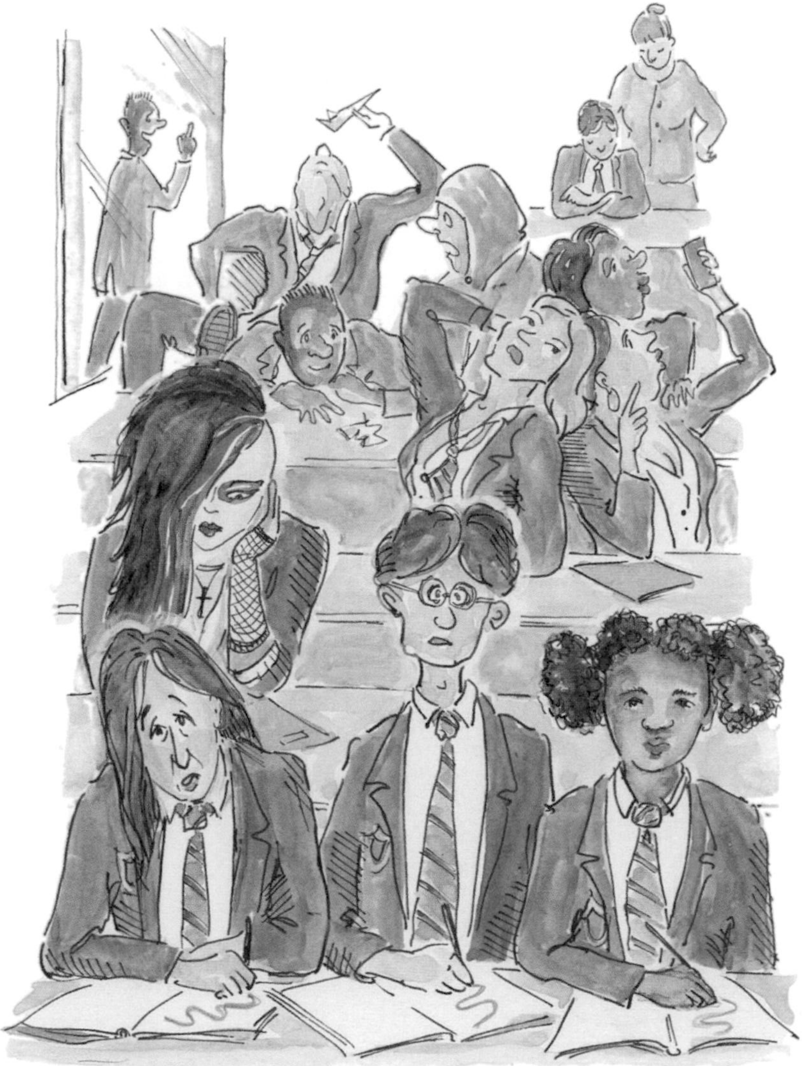

*age 14–15

IDENTIFICATION CHART
(juveniles)

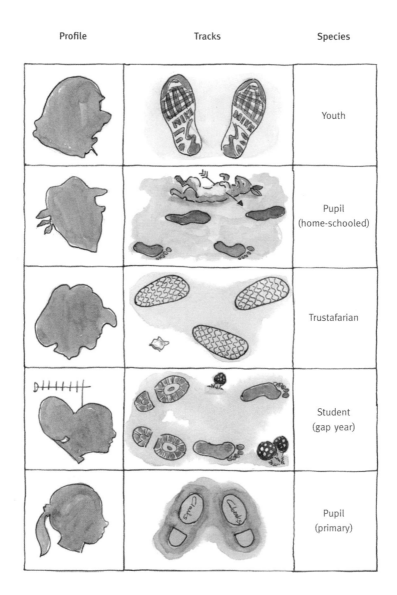

Profile	Tracks	Species
		Youth
		Pupil (home-schooled)
		Trustafarian
		Student (gap year)
		Pupil (primary)

Variations in plumage:

LADIES WHO LUNCH / PERSONAL TRAINER
INTERIOR DESIGNER / NEW AGE PENSIONER
LANDED GENTRY / OLIGARCH [exotic]

LADIES WHO LUNCH

filled
♀
botched
tucked
lifted

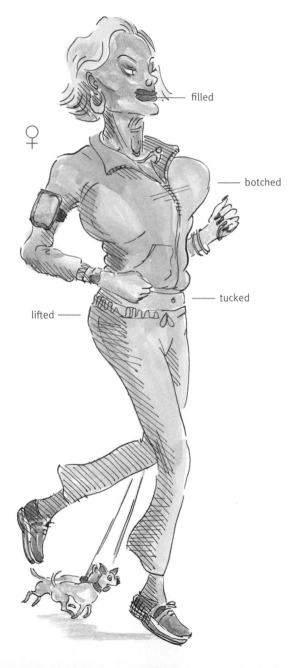

Primary facial expressions:

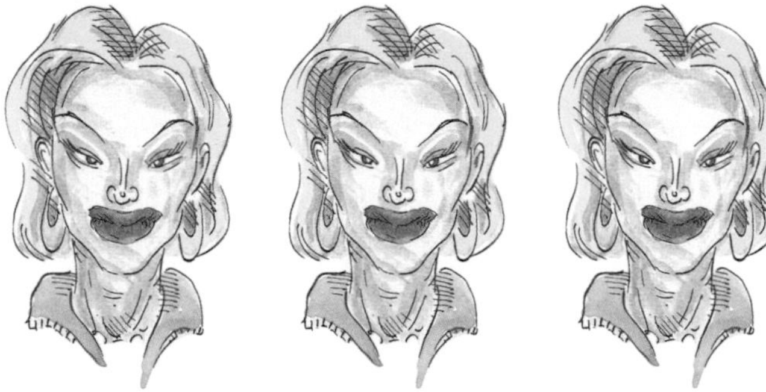

bored bitchy bemused

Flocking:

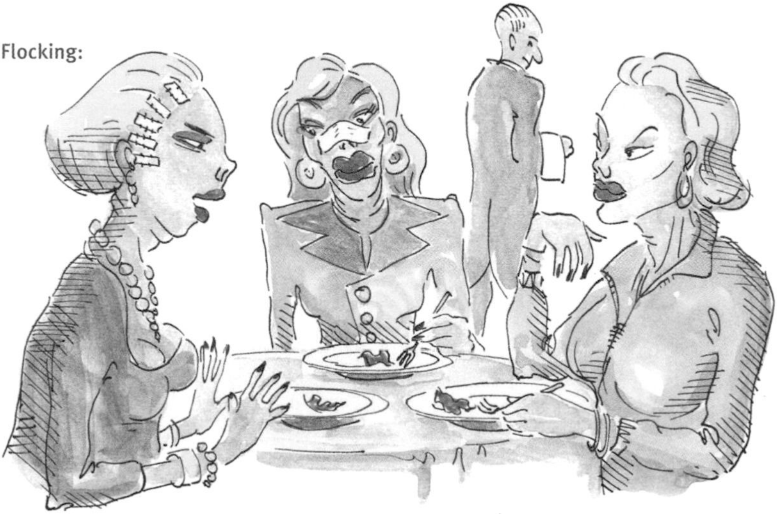

Staple diet:

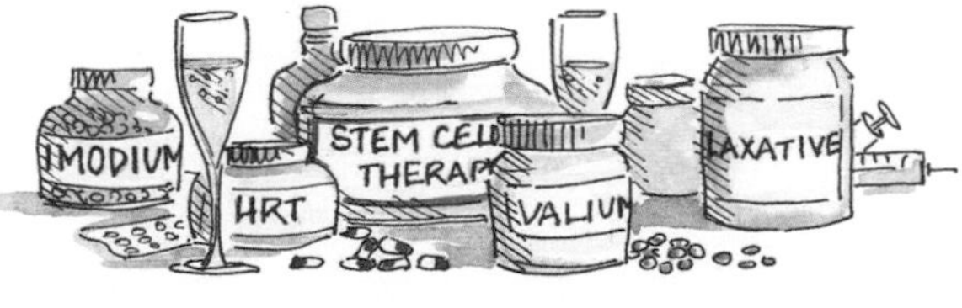
IMODIUM
STEM CEL
THERAP
HRT
VALIU
LAXATIVE

Distribution:

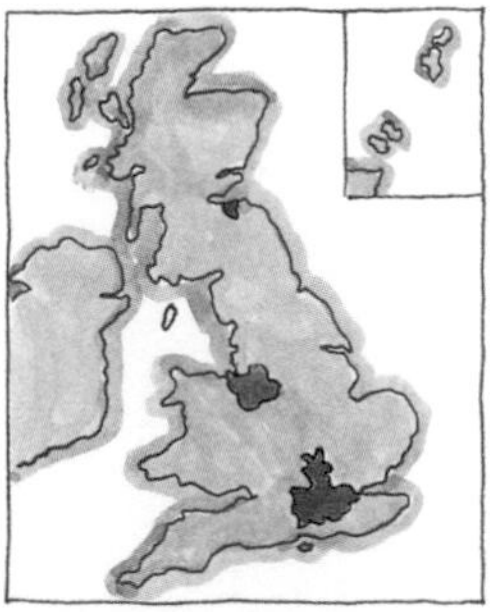

PERSONAL TRAINER

♂

—— top-heavy

Interaction with other species:

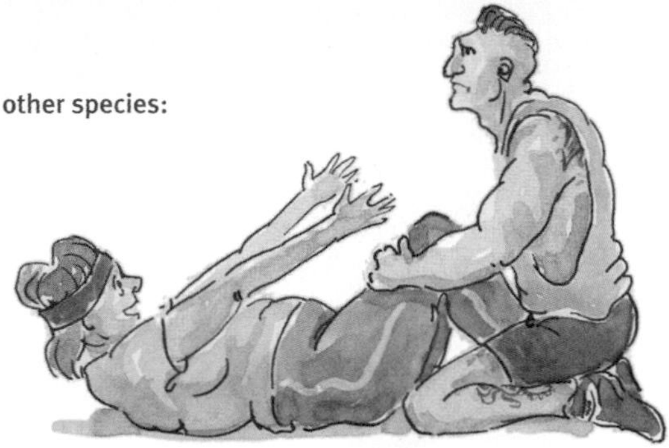

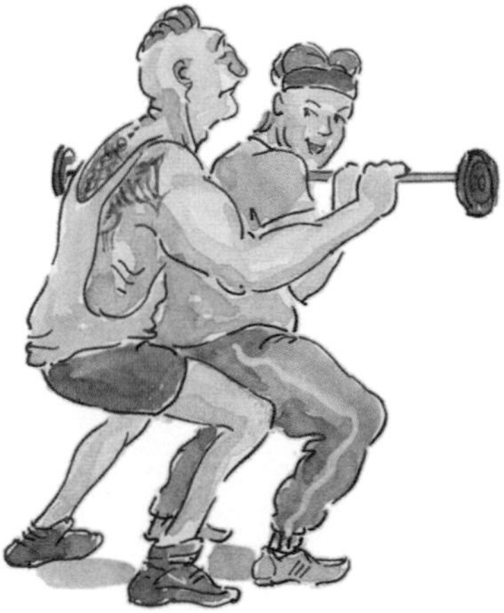

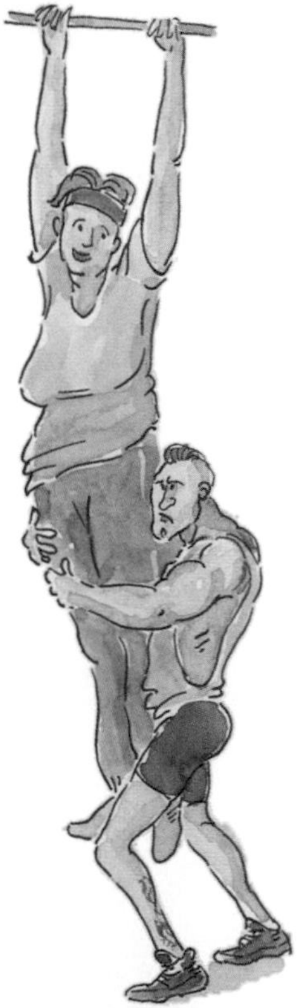

Mate:

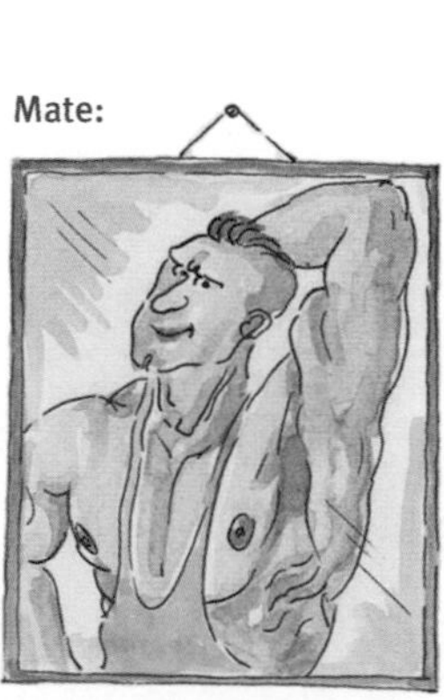

Staple diet:

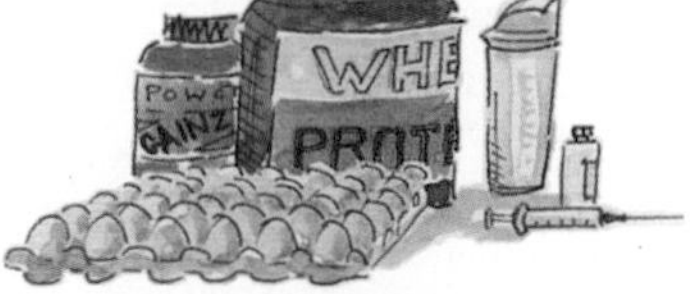
WHE
PROT

INTERIOR DESIGNER

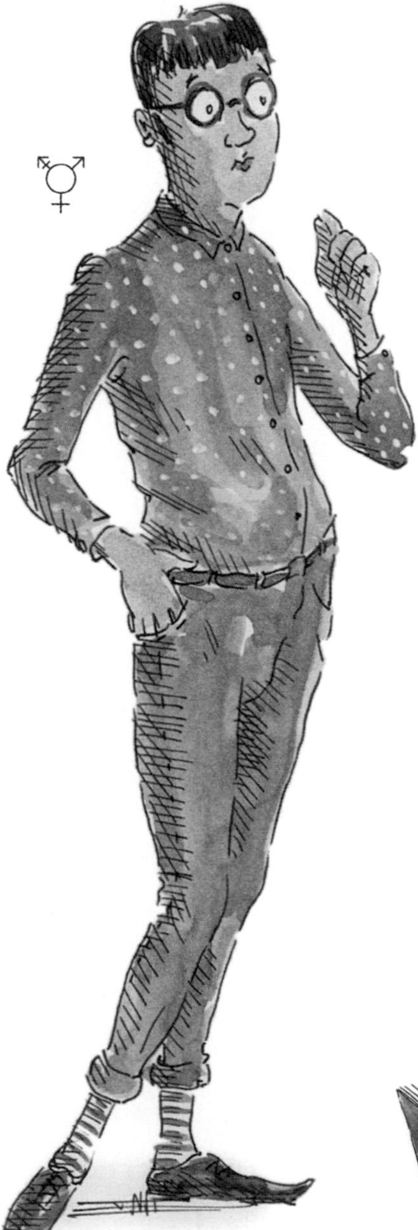

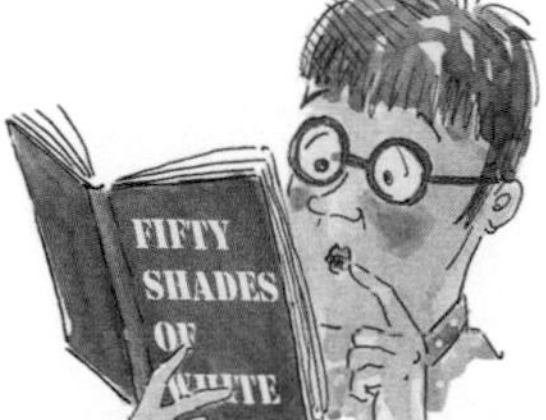
FIFTY
SHADES
OF

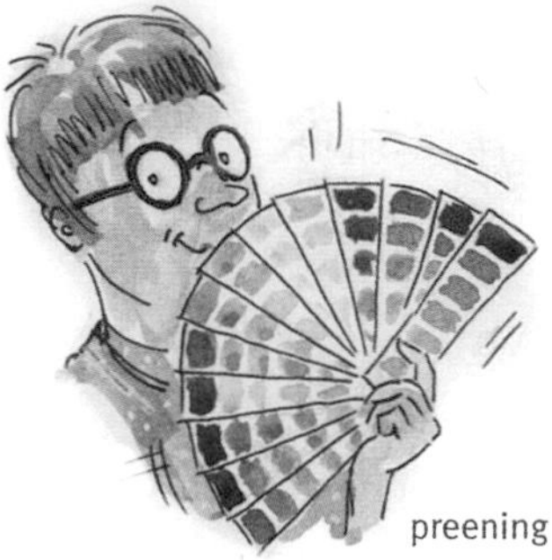

preening

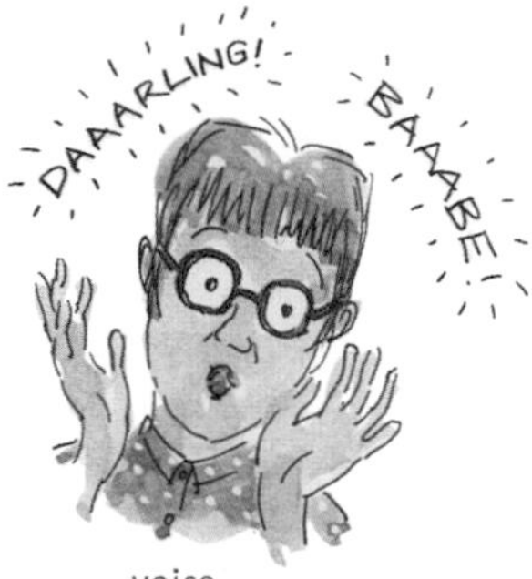
DAAARLING!
BAAABE!

voice

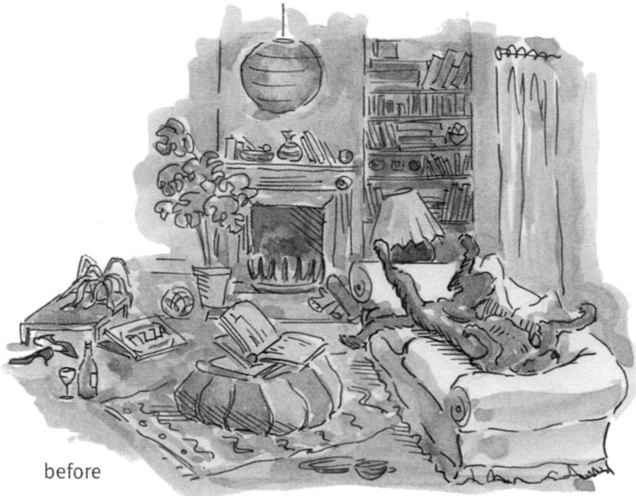
PIZZA

before

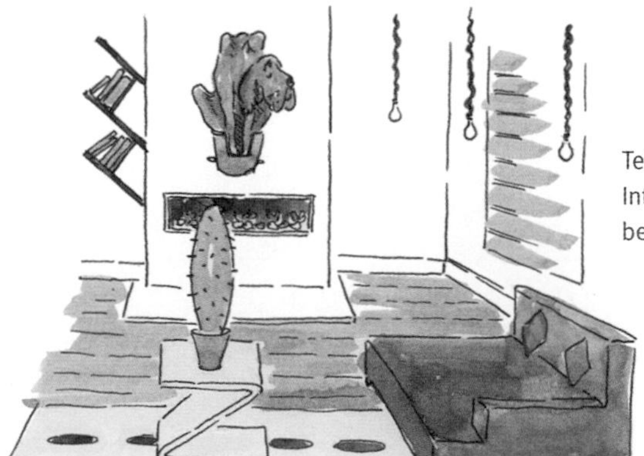

after

Telltale signs that an Interior Designer has been in your house

NEW AGE PENSIONER

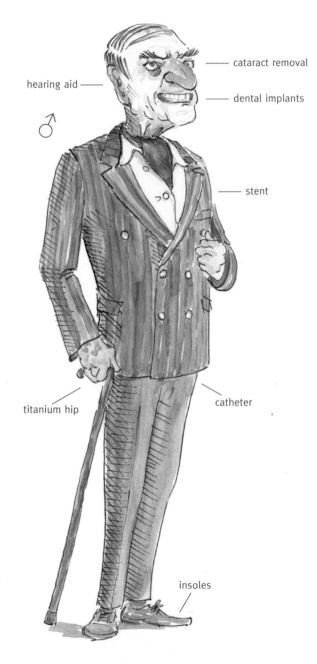

cataract removal

hearing aid

dental implants

♂

stent

titanium hip

catheter

insoles

Mating call:

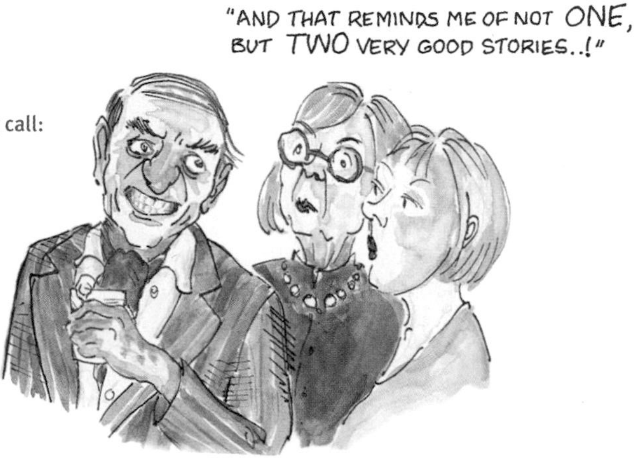
"AND THAT REMINDS ME OF NOT ONE, BUT TWO VERY GOOD STORIES..!"

Mating display:

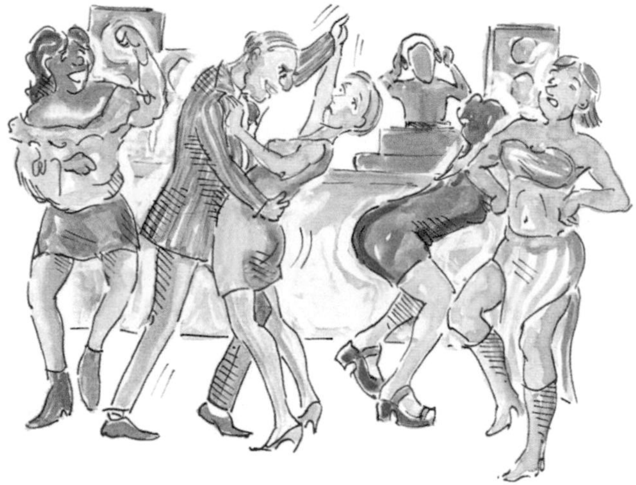

Flocking:

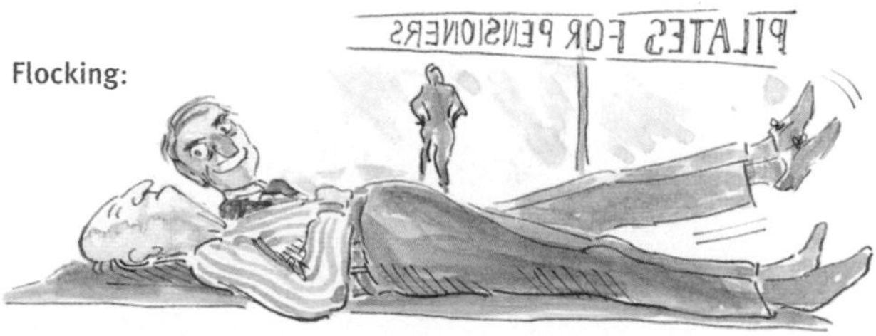
PILATES FOR PENSIONERS

LANDED GENTRY

noble

♀

duck-like walk

Mate:

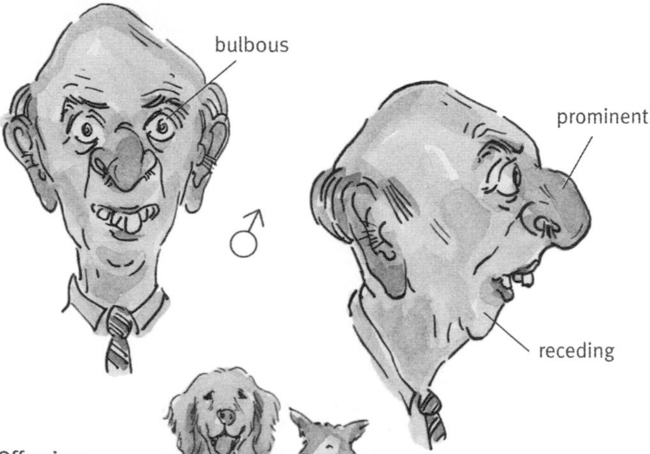
bulbous
prominent
♂
receding

Offspring:

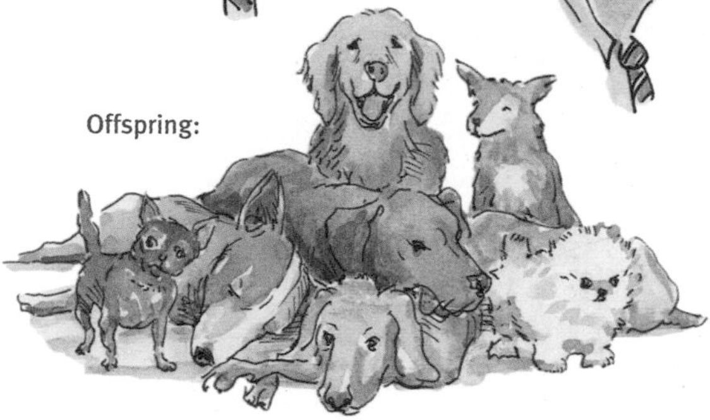

Observing Landed Gentry in the field:

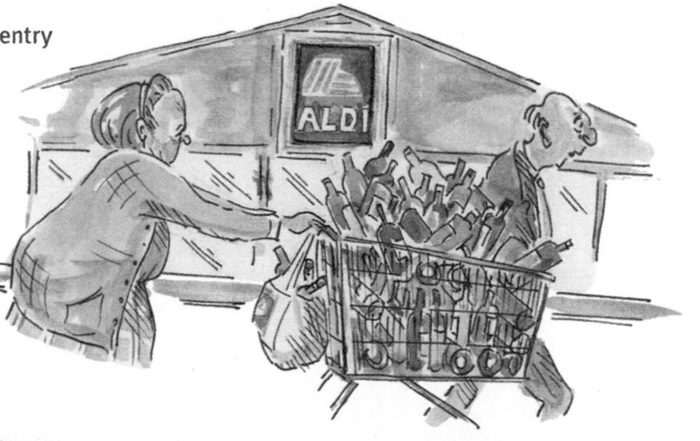
ALDI

Habitat:

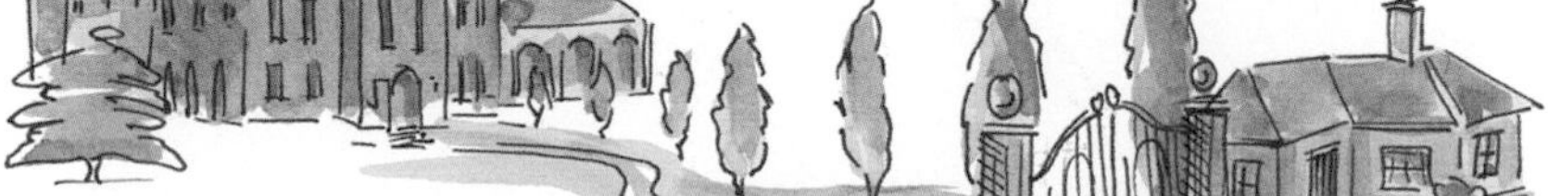

Either house, depending on financial circumstances

OLIGARCH

Mate:
♀

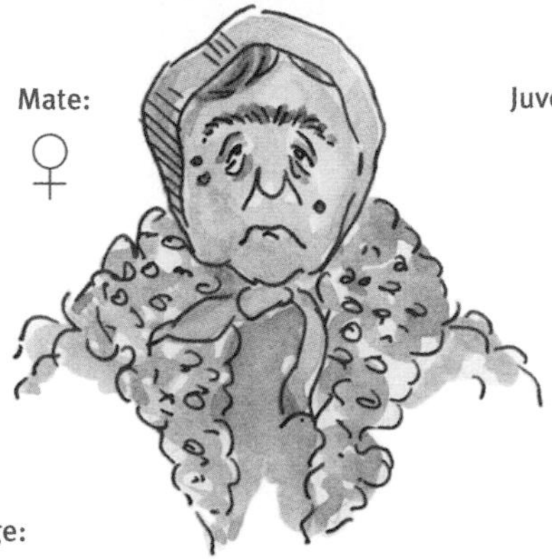

Juvenile:

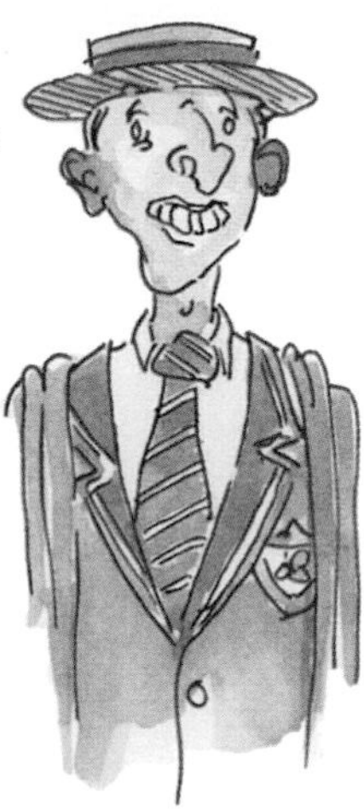

Camouflage:

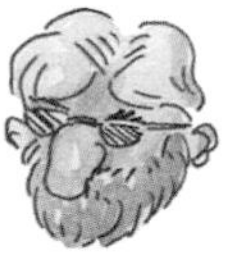

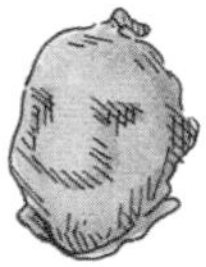

Behaviour:
with unknown ♀

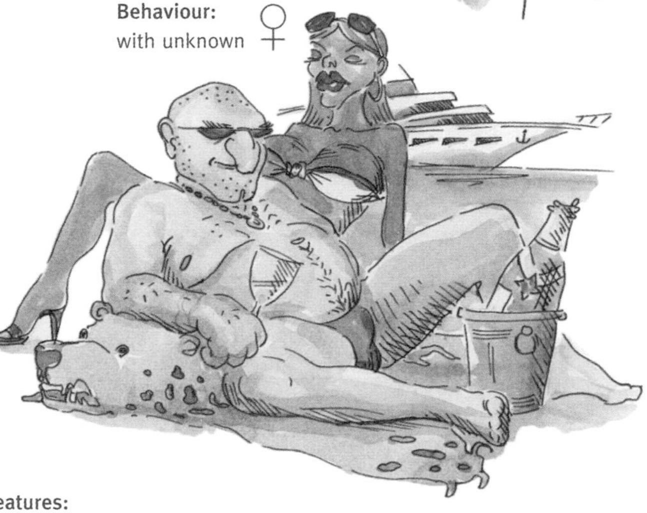

Distinguishing features:

bushy
hooded

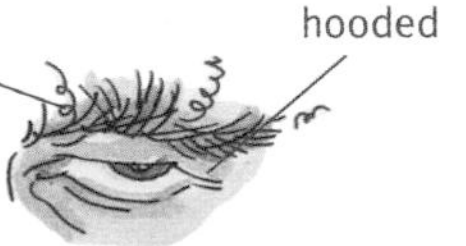

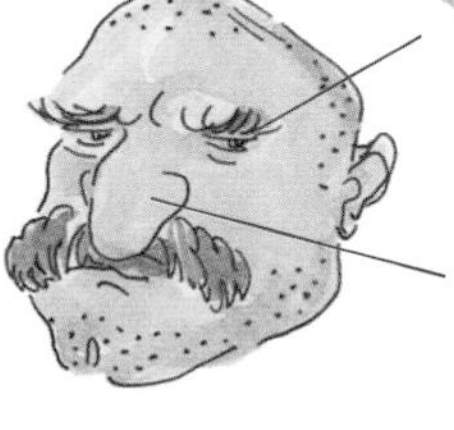

nose profiles

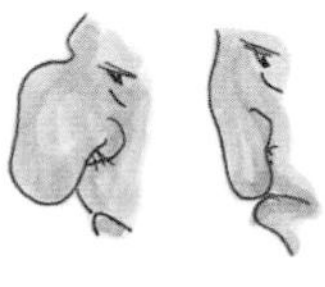

pallid skin due to diet of vodka, caviar and toxins

Distribution:

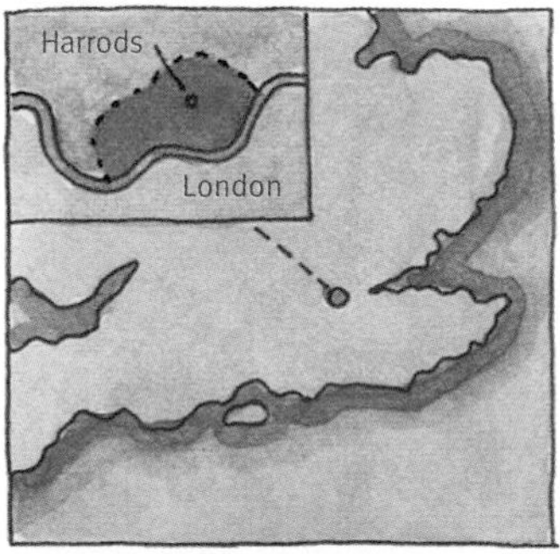
Harrods
London

IDENTIFICATION CHART
(exotic)

Profile	Tracks	Species
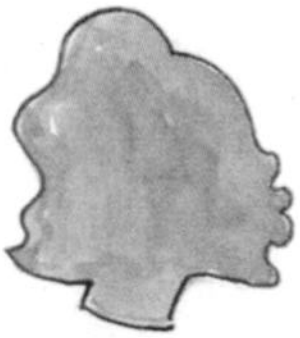	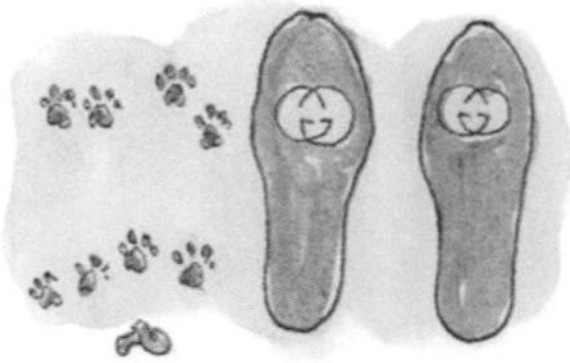	Ladies Who Lunch
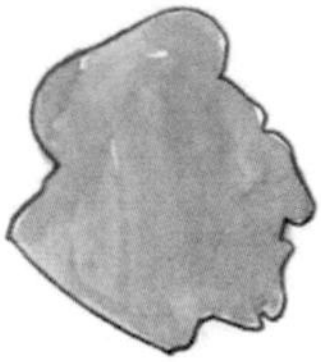	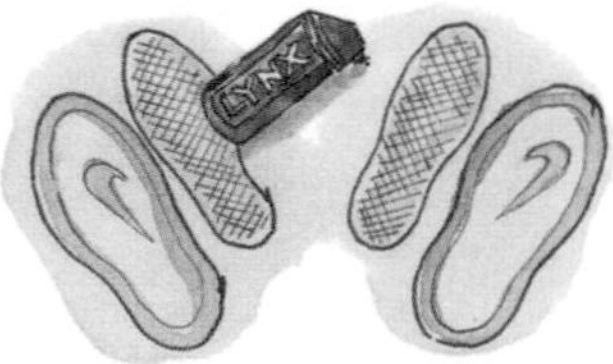	Personal Trainer
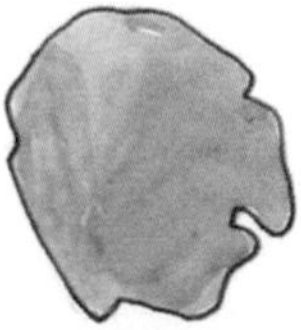	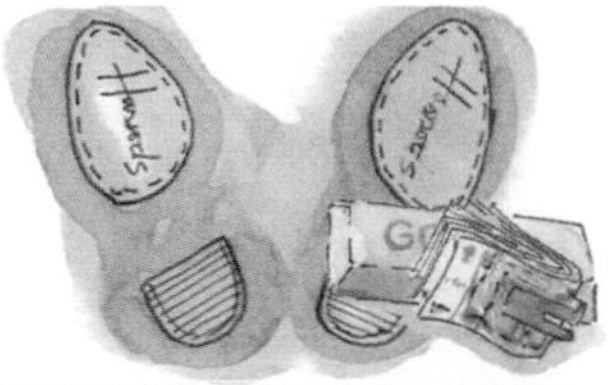	Oligarch
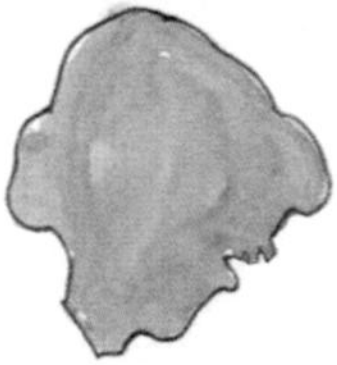	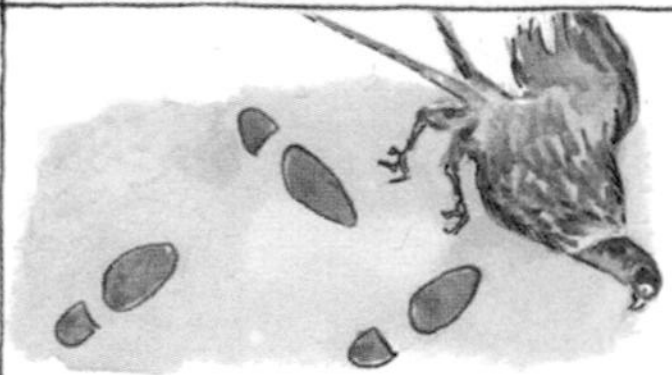	Landed Gentry ♂
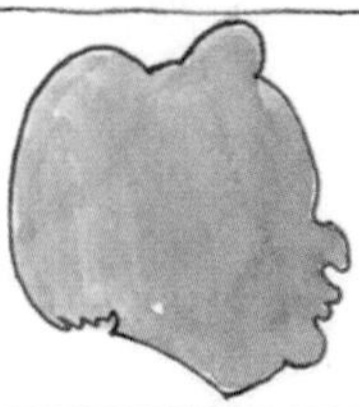	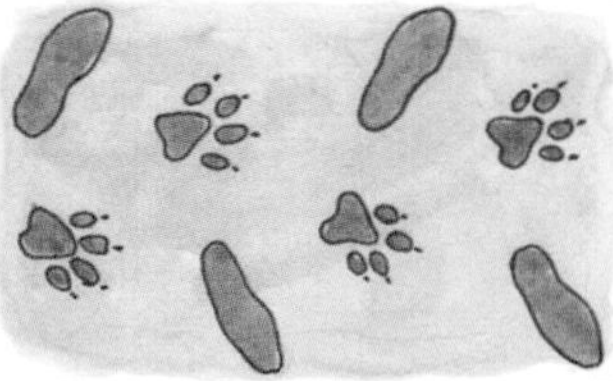	Landed Gentry ♀

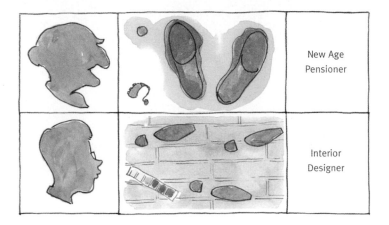

| | | New Age Pensioner |
| | | Interior Designer |

Population:

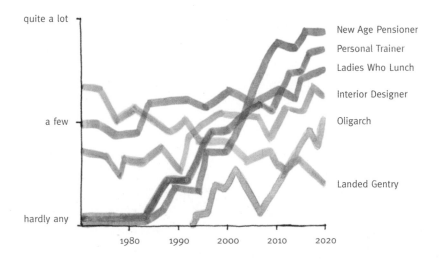

quite a lot — New Age Pensioner
Personal Trainer
Ladies Who Lunch

Interior Designer

a few — Oligarch

Landed Gentry

hardly any —

1980   1990   2000   2010   2020

DFL / TRAFFIC WARDEN / COUGAR / CELEBRITY
PROPERTY DEVELOPER / "LIFESTYLE" SHOPKEEPER [pest]

DFL (Down From London)

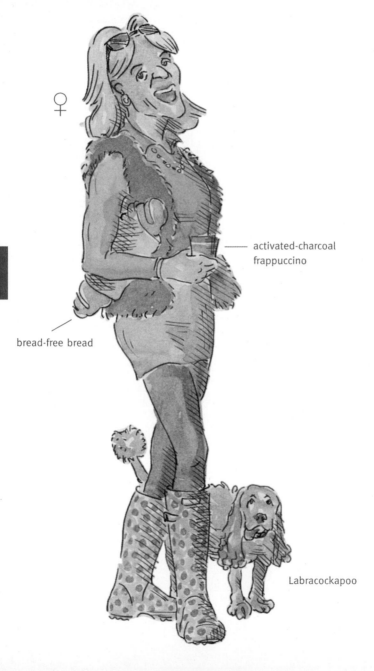

♀

activated-charcoal frappuccino

bread-free bread

Labracockapoo

Observing a DFL in the field:

Local species

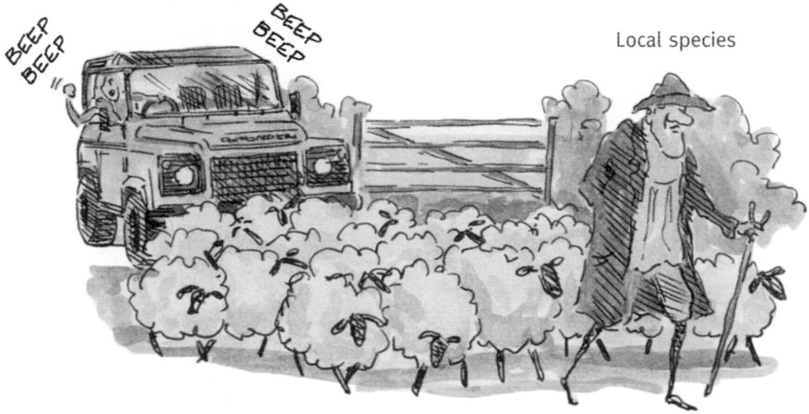
BEEP
BEEP
BEEP
BEEP

Behaviour:

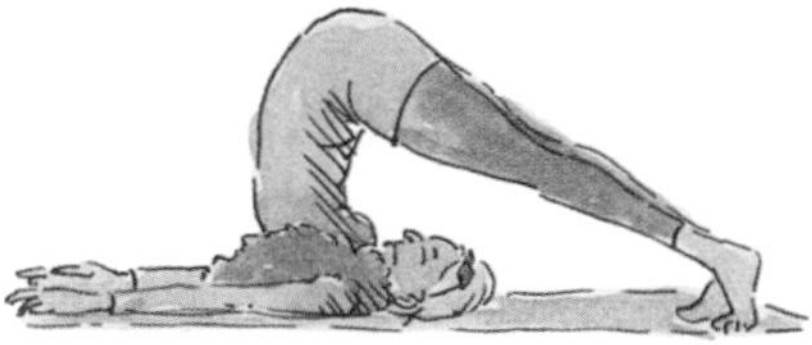

a.m.

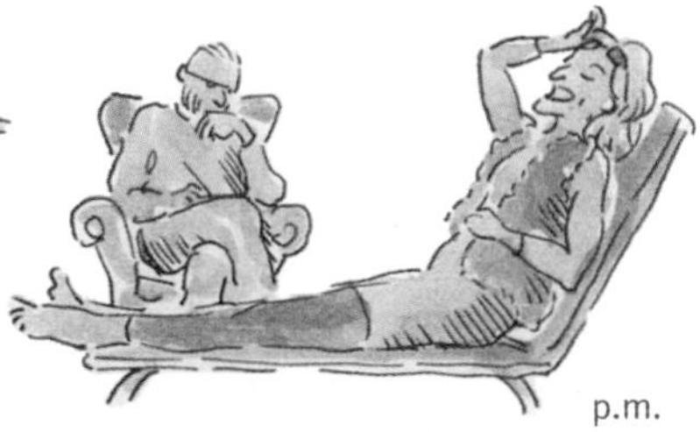

p.m.

Cross-species contact:

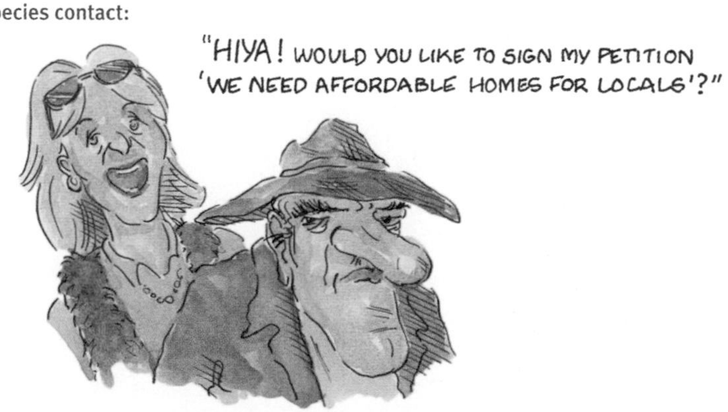
"HIYA! WOULD YOU LIKE TO SIGN MY PETITION
'WE NEED AFFORDABLE HOMES FOR LOCALS'?"

TRAFFIC WARDEN

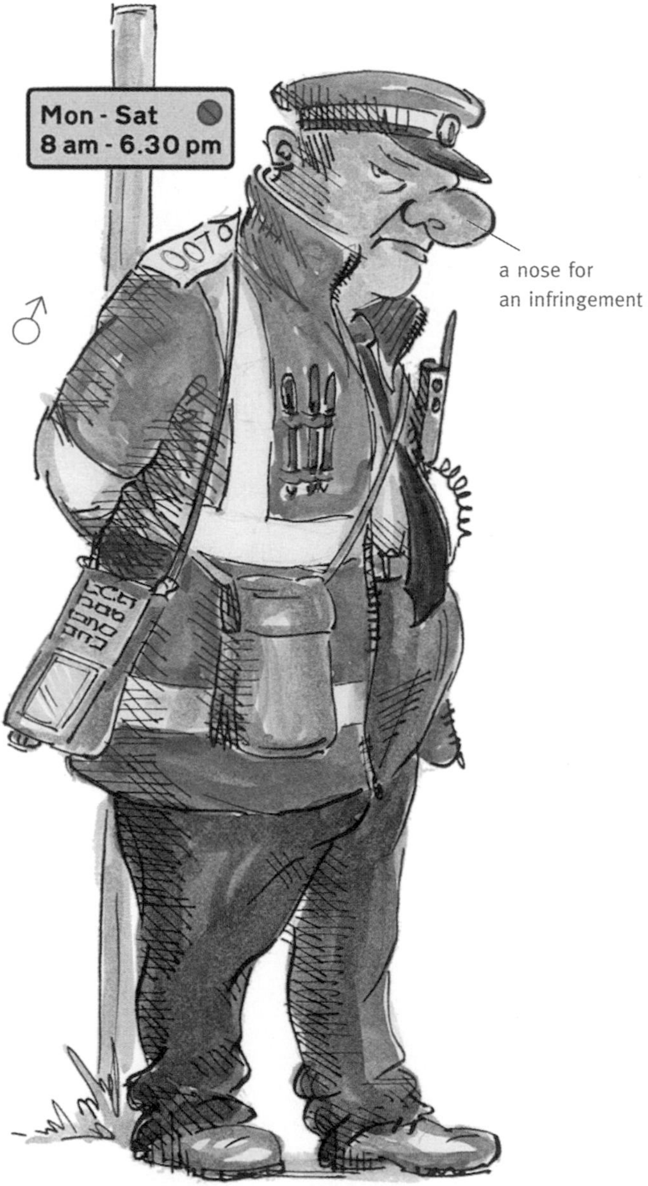
Mon - Sat
8 am - 6.30 pm
a nose for
an infringement
♂

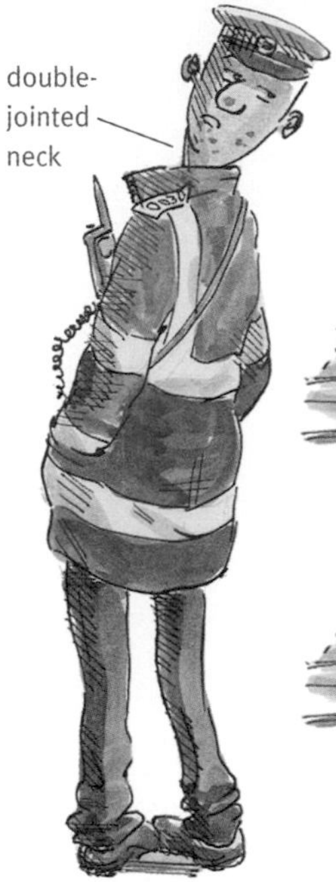
double-
jointed
neck

Observing a Traffic Warden in the field:

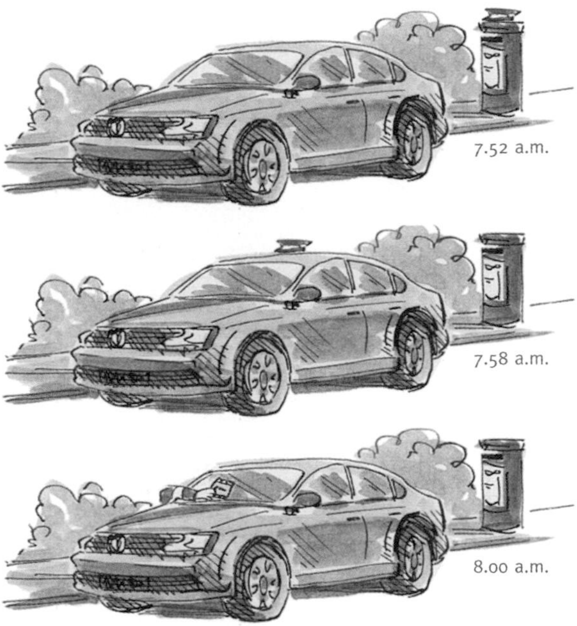
7.52 a.m.
7.58 a.m.
8.00 a.m.

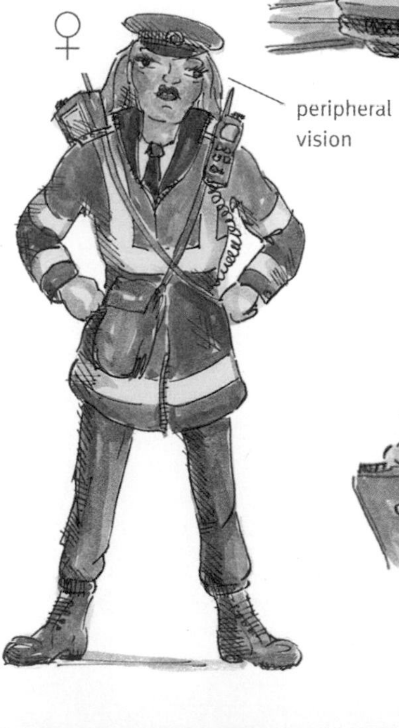
♀
peripheral
vision

Interaction with other species:

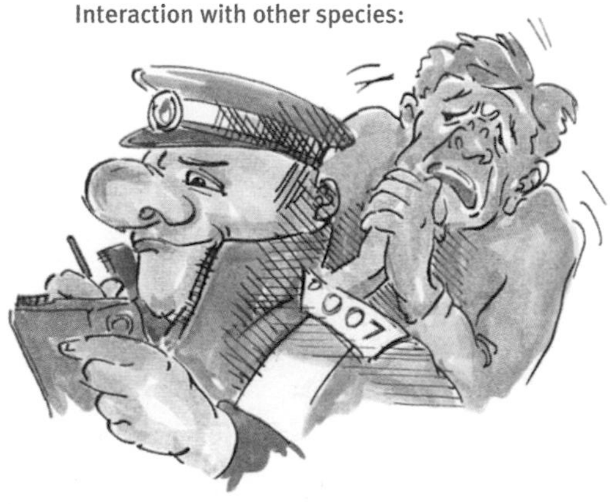
007

COUGAR

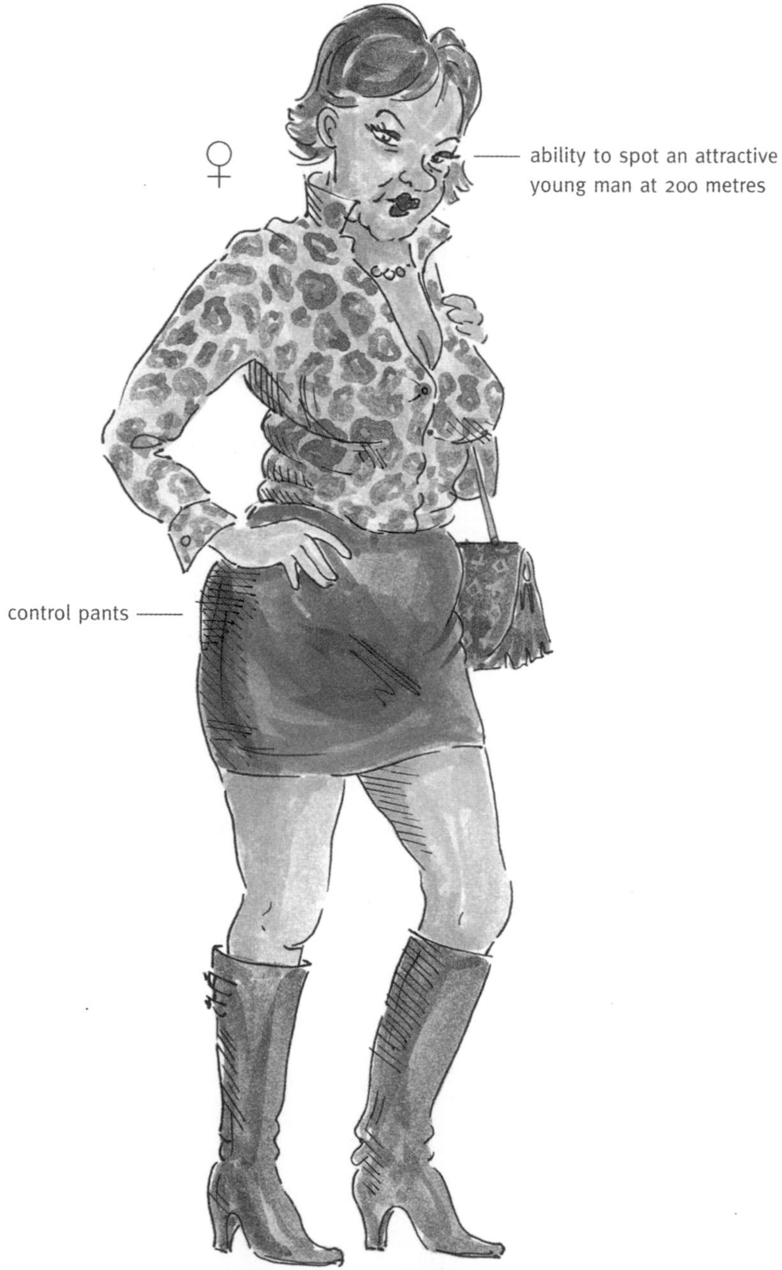
♀
ability to spot an attractive young man at 200 metres
control pants

Staple diet:

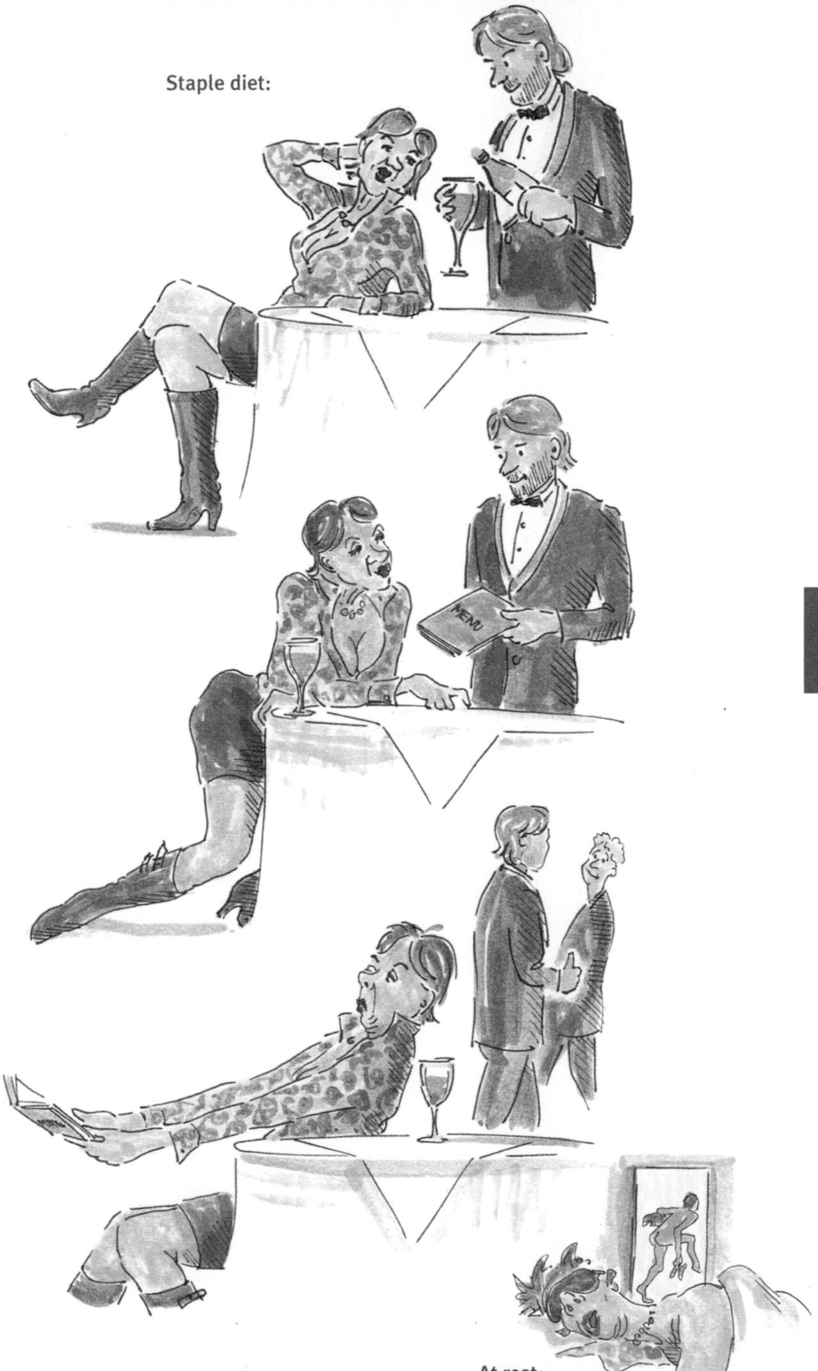

MENU

At rest:

CELEBRITY

♀

real feelings

Attention-seeking behaviour:

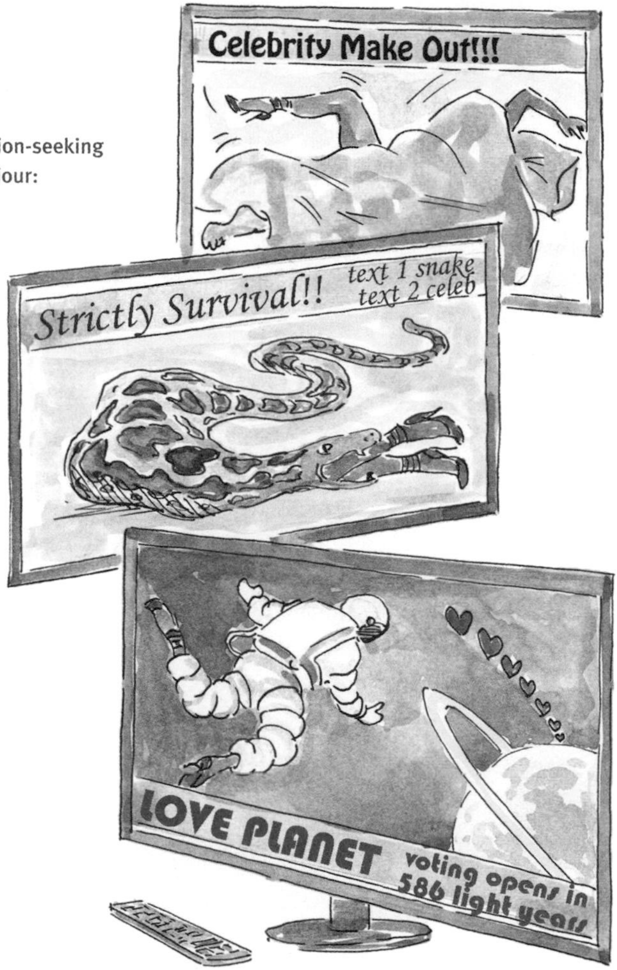
Celebrity Make Out!!!
Strictly Survival!!
text 1 snake
text 2 celeb
LOVE PLANET
voting opens in
586 light years

Habitat:

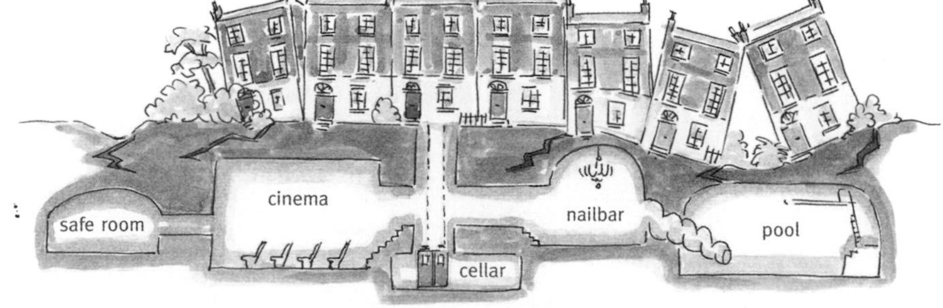
safe room
cinema
cellar
nailbar
pool

PROPERTY DEVELOPER

Behaviour:

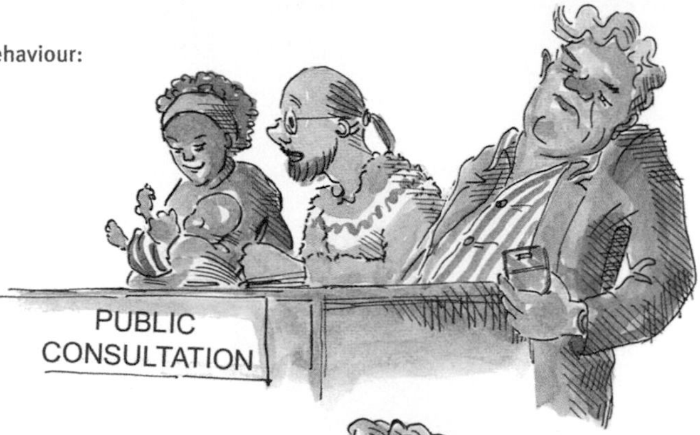
PUBLIC
CONSULTATION

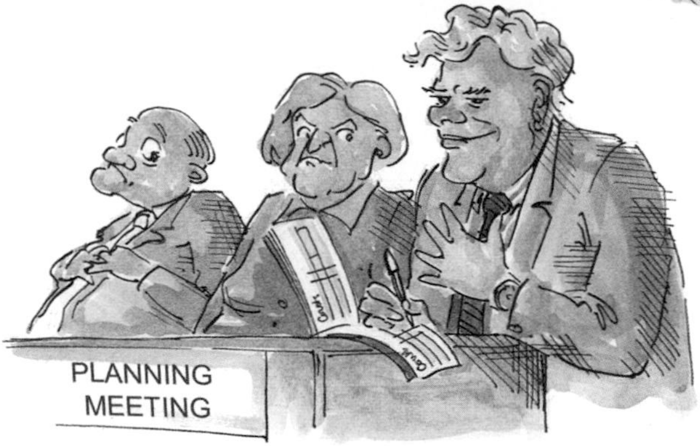
PLANNING
MEETING

Telltale signs that a Property Developer has been in the area

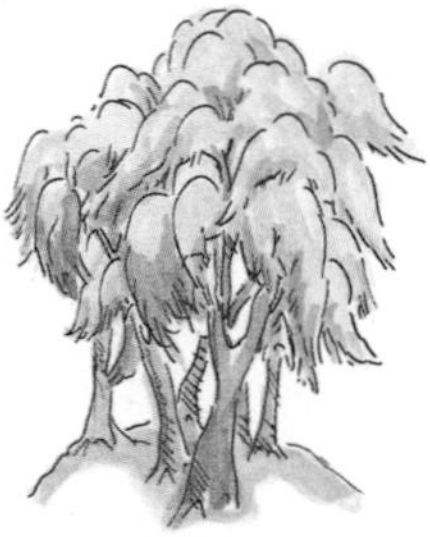

before

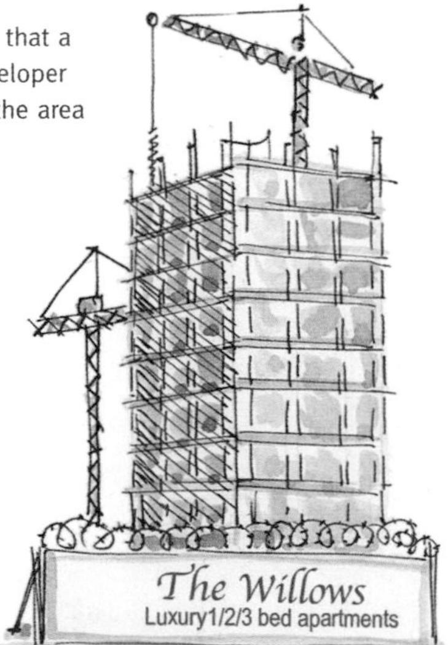
The Willows
Luxury1/2/3 bed apartments

after

Deterrent:

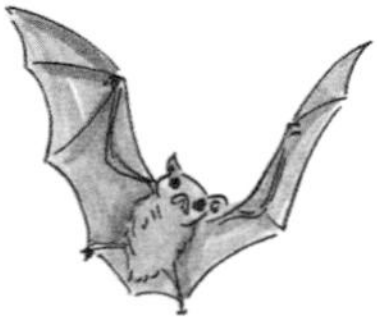

rare bats

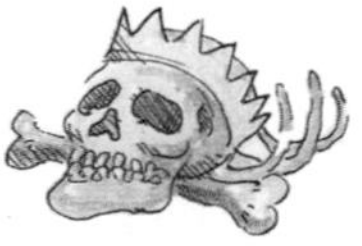

archaeological remains

"LIFESTYLE" SHOPKEEPER

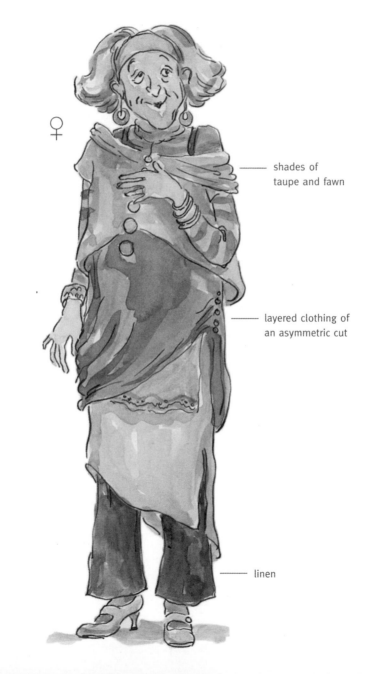

shades of
taupe and fawn

layered clothing of
an asymmetric cut

linen

Mate:

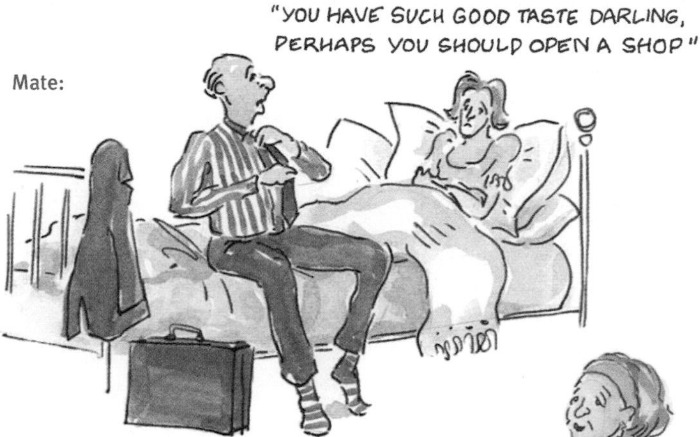
"YOU HAVE SUCH GOOD TASTE DARLING,
PERHAPS YOU SHOULD OPEN A SHOP"

Habitat:

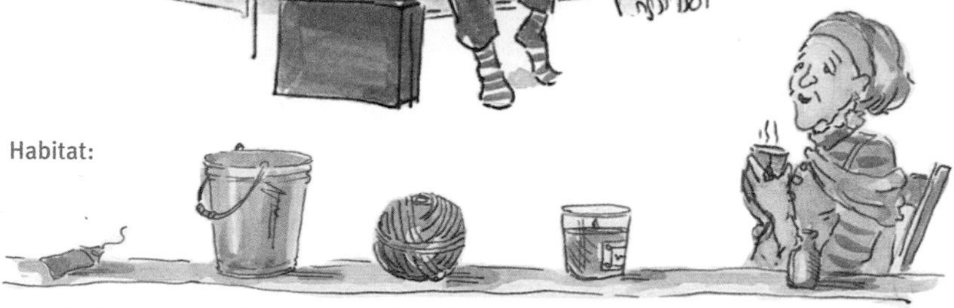

sustainably cut, organic eco-labels	hand-distressed vintage bucket	lifestyle string	patchouli and truffle-scented candle with goldleaf flakes	ethically infused kefir chai

Flocking:

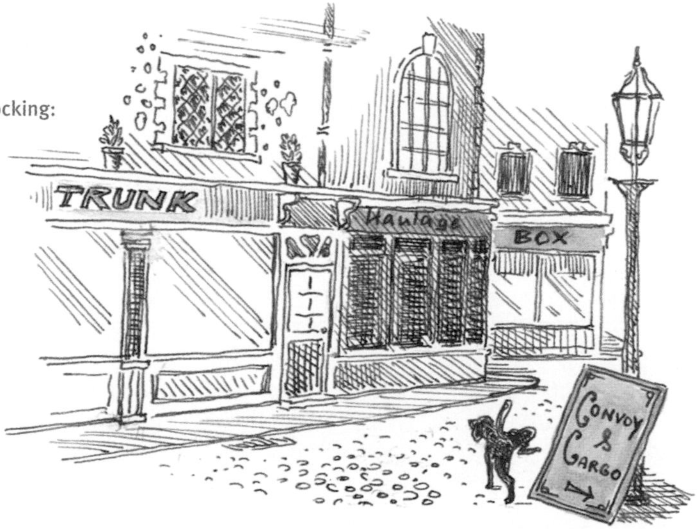
TRUNK
Haulage
BOX
CONVOY & CARGO

Can be observed along the high streets of affluent towns, in premises previously occupied by butchers, tailors, locksmiths, etc.

IDENTIFICATION CHART
(pest)

Profile	Tracks	Species

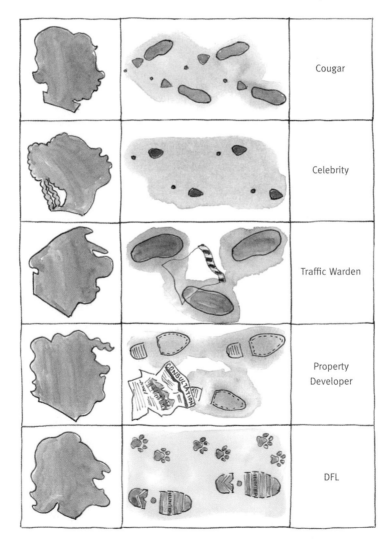

		Cougar
		Celebrity
		Traffic Warden
		Property Developer
		DFL

Distribution:

"Lifestyle" Shopkeeper	DFL
Celebrity	Property Developer
Cougar	Traffic Warden

BRITS FROM BEHIND
SCREEN ADDICTS
LOCAL CHOIR
INTERSPECIES GATHERING
FUTURE BRITONS
STAYCATIONERS
COMMUTERS

(miscellaneous)

BRITS FROM BEHIND
(mamil*)

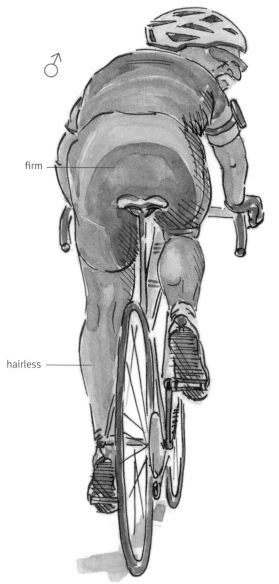

firm

hairless

*middle-aged man in Lycra

(plumber)

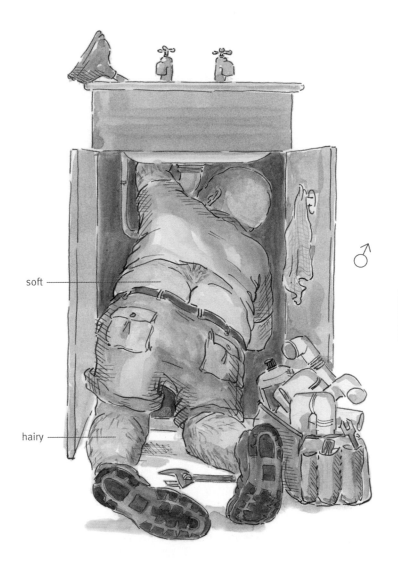

soft

hairy

♂

(farmer)

Distribution:

(caravan man)

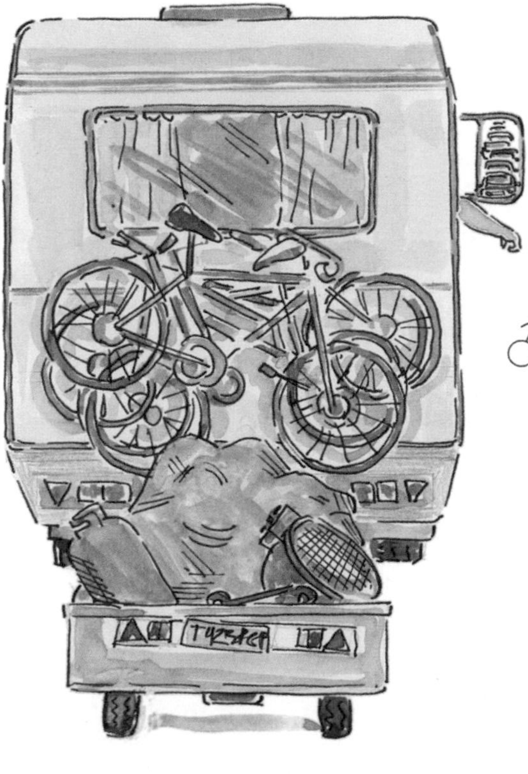
TIPSTER

♂

Distribution:

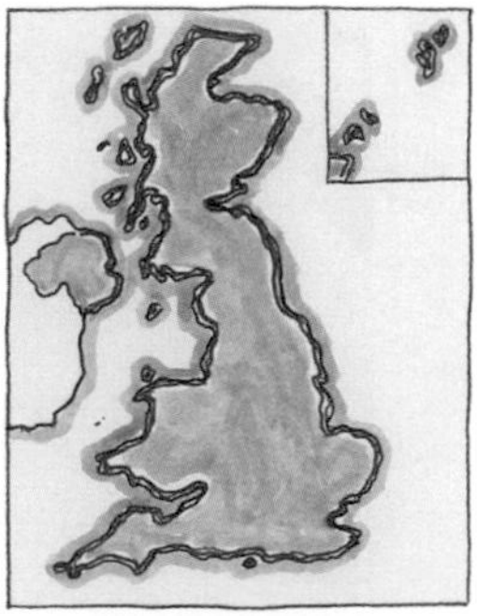

SCREEN ADDICTS*

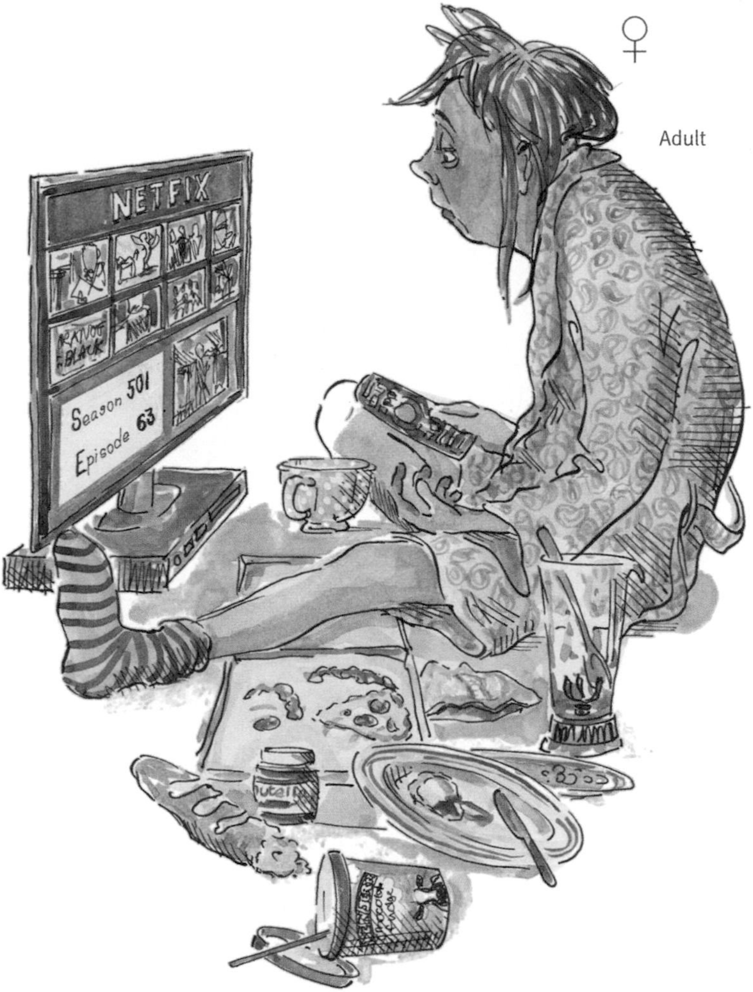
NETFIX
Season 501
Episode 63

♀

Adult

*social media addicts: Foodie, Pupil (secondary), Commuters

Juvenile

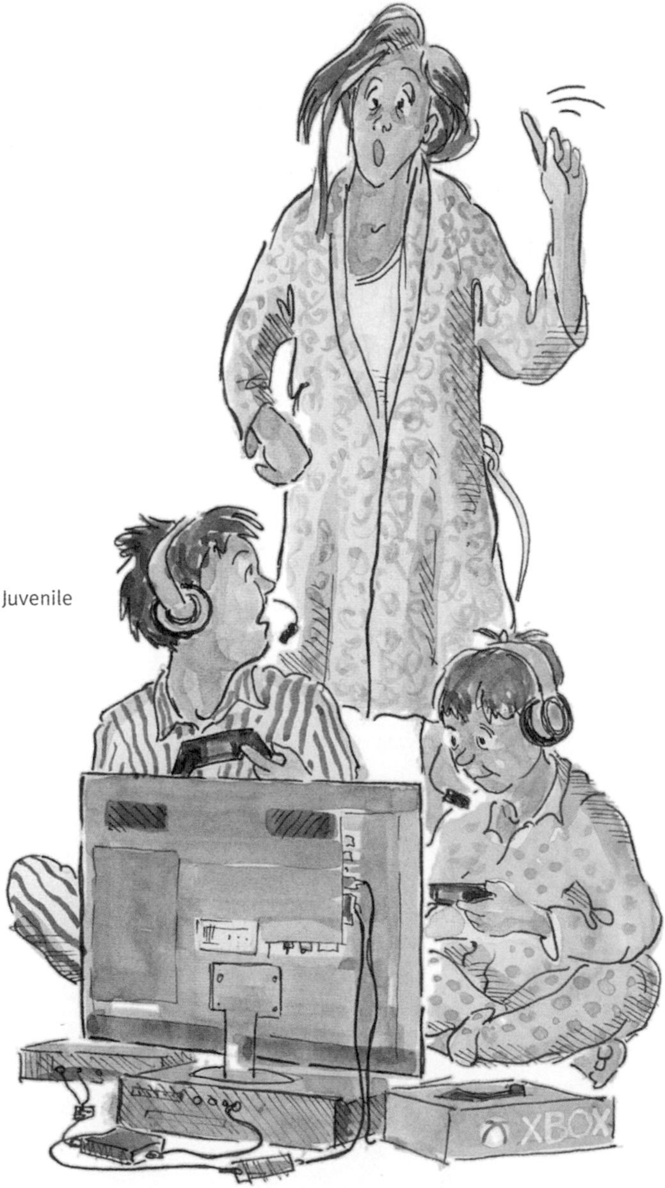
XBOX

LOCAL CHOIR

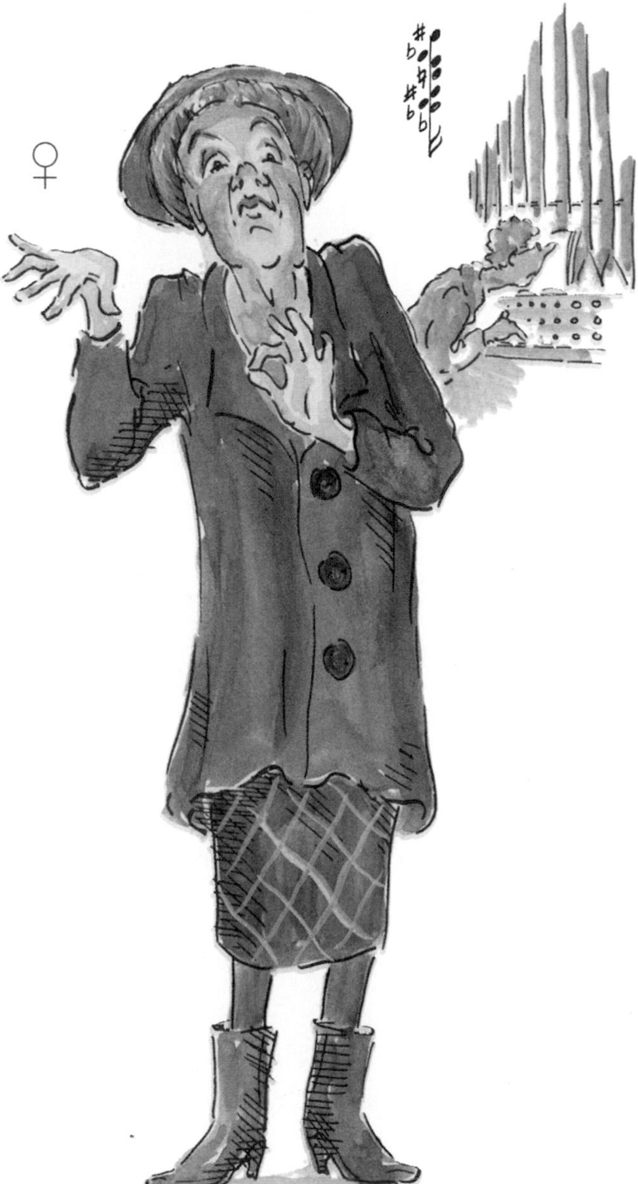

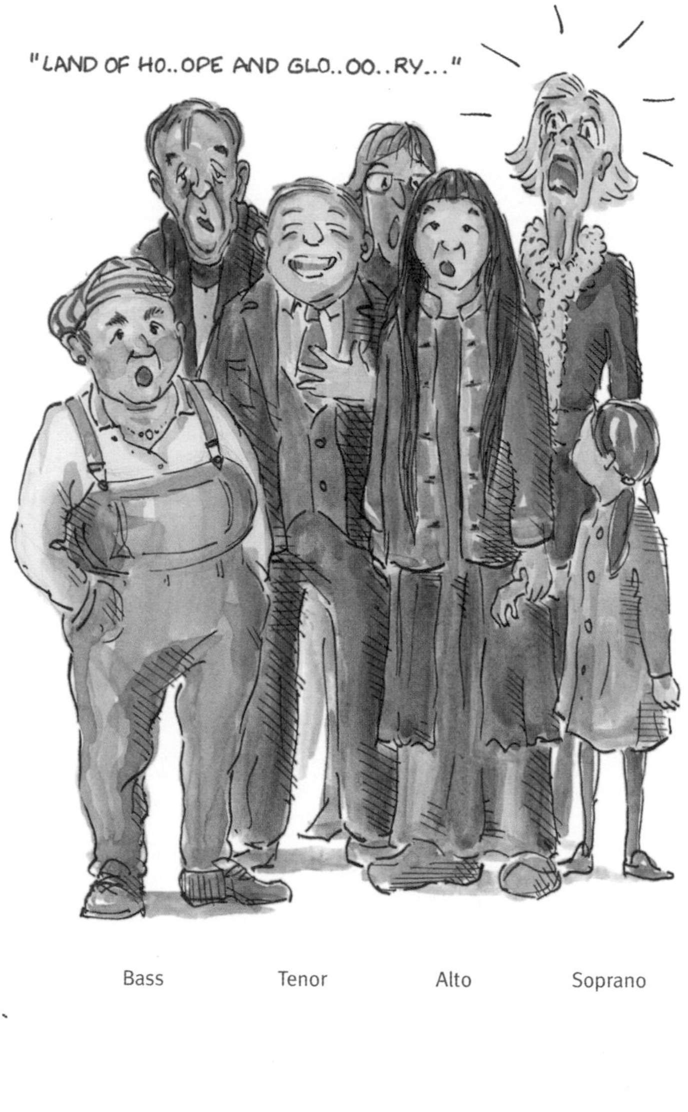
"LAND OF HO..OPE AND GLO..OO..RY..."

Bass Tenor Alto Soprano

INTERSPECIES GATHERING

♂

Instructor

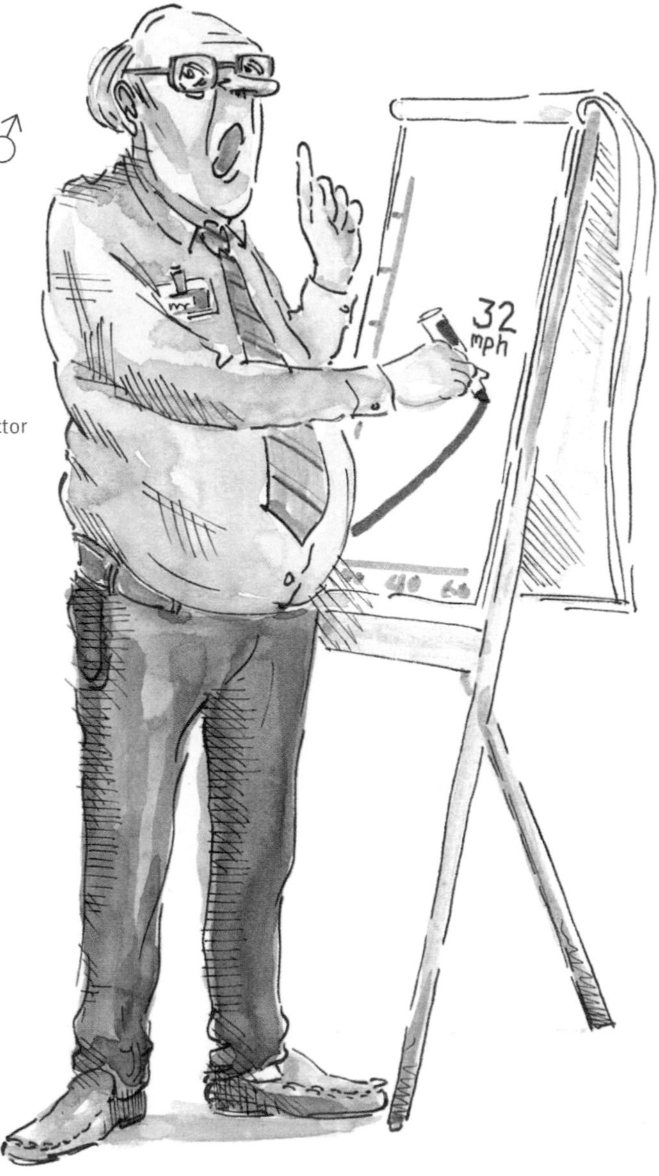

32
mph

Speed awareness course

FUTURE BRITONS

A species of manual labourers expected to evolve with the possible departure of "low-skilled" immigrants

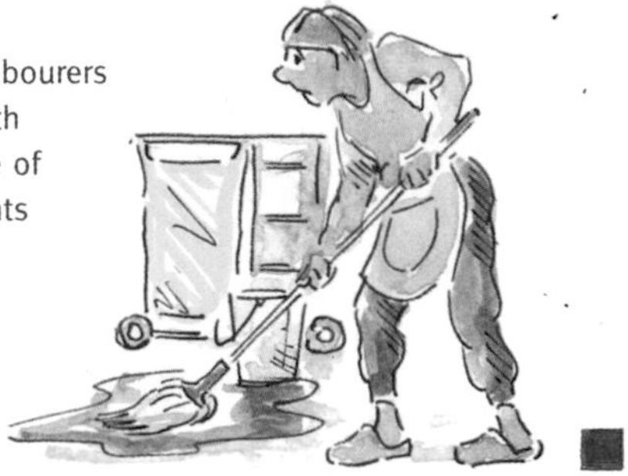

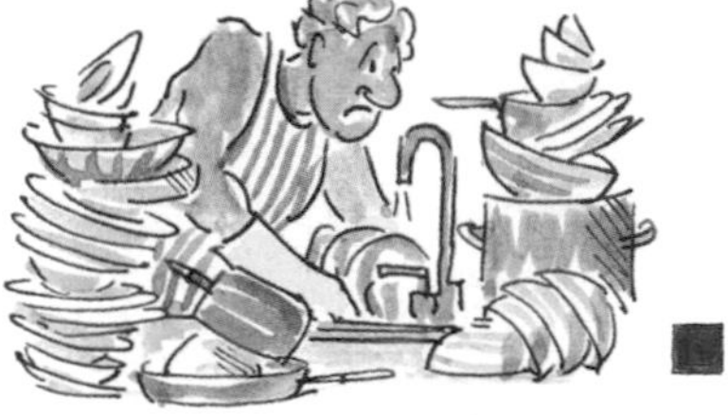

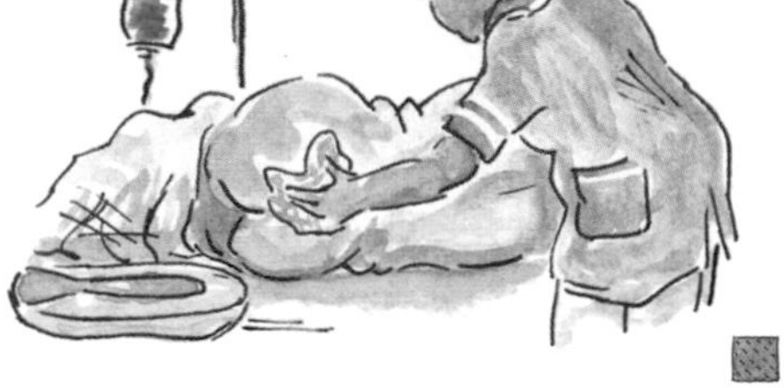

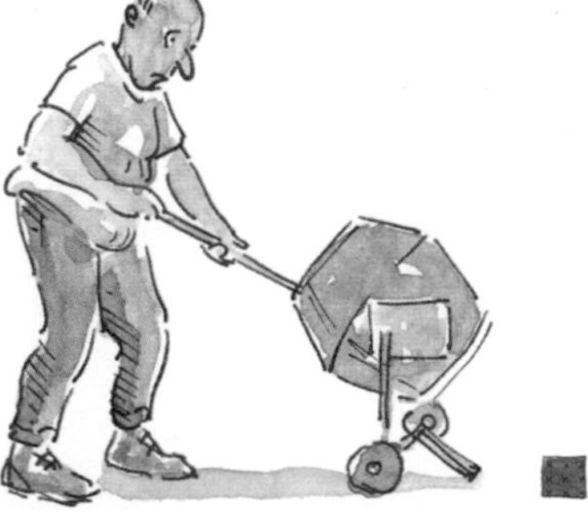

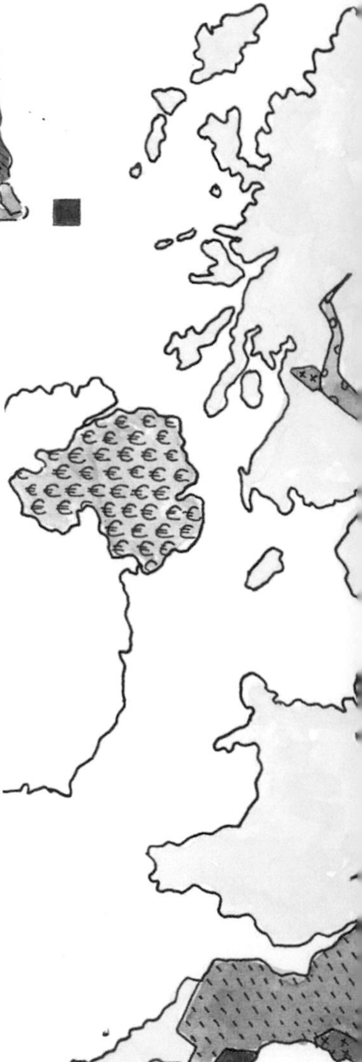